STAGING PRISON THEATRE IN CANADA

STAGING PRISON THEATRE IN CANADA

Setting the Spotlight on William Head on Stage

Thana Ridha and Sylvie Frigon

University of Ottawa Press
2025

 Les **Presses** de l'Université d'Ottawa
University of Ottawa **Press**

Les Presses de l'Université d'Ottawa / University of Ottawa Press (PUO-UOP) is North America's flagship bilingual university press, affiliated to one of Canada's top research universities. PUO-UOP enriches the intellectual and cultural discourse of our increasingly knowledge-based and globalized world with peer-reviewed, award-winning books.

www.Press.uOttawa.ca

Library and Archives Canada Cataloguing in Publication

Title: Staging prison theatre in Canada : setting the spotlight on William Head on Stage / Thana Ridha and Sylvie Frigon.
Names: Ridha, Thana, author. | Frigon, Sylvie, author
Description: Includes bibliographical references and index.
Identifiers: Canadiana (print) 20250114305 | Canadiana (ebook) 20250114313 | ISBN 9780776644905 (softcover) | ISBN 9780776644912 (hardcover) | ISBN 9780776644929 (ePUB) | ISBN 9780776644936 (PDF)
Subjects: LCSH: William Head on Stage (Theater company)—History. | LCSH: Prison theater—Canada—History. | LCSH: Prisoners—Services for—Canada—History. | LCSH: Theatrical companies—Canada—History.
Classification: LCC HV8861.R53 2025 | DDC 365/.668—dc23

Legal Deposit: Second Quarter 2025
Library and Archives Canada

© Thana Ridha and Sylvie Frigon 2025
All rights reserved

Creative Commons Open Access Licence
Attribution-Non-Commercial-Share Alike 4.0 International (CC BY-NC-ND 4.0)
By virtue of this licence you are free to:
Share—copy and redistribute the material in any medium or format
Attribution—You must give appropriate credit, provide a link to the license, and indicate if changes were made. You may do so in any reasonable manner, but not in any way that suggests the licensor endorses you or your use.
Non-Commercial—You may not use the material for commercial purposes.
No Derivatives—If you remix, transform, or build upon the material, you may not distribute the modified material.
No additional restrictions—You may not apply legal terms or technological measures that legally restrict others from doing anything the license permits.

Production Team
Copy editing   Valentina D'Aliesio
Proofreading   Tanina Drvar
Typesetting   Nord Compo
Cover design   Benoit Deneault

Cover Image   Inmate and artist performing in William Head on Stage's 2014 production, *Time Waits for No One*. Photograph: Jam Hamidi, for William Head on Stage.

We would like to acknowledge funding support from the Collabzium "Always Be Closing" Grant from the Faculty of Social Sciences, University of Ottawa.

This research was partly supported by the Social Sciences and Humanities Research Council of Canada (SSHRC), the Ontario Graduate Scholarship (OGS), as well as support from the University of Ottawa's Faculty Research Chair: The Prison in Culture, Culture in Prison.

---

 uOttawa

PUO-UOP gratefully acknowledges the funding support of the University of Ottawa, the Government of Canada, the Canada Council for the Arts, the Ontario Arts Council and the Government of Ontario.

Table of Contents

List of Figures vii

List of Tables ix

Foreword
Kate Rubin and Jeni Luther xi

Acknowledgements xv

CHAPTER 1
The Opening Script 1
   1.1. Narrating the WHoS Story 3
   1.2. Narrating the Experiences with WHoS 6
   1.3. Positionality 9
   1.4. Organization of the Book 14

CHAPTER 2
Setting the Stage 17
   2.1. Approaches to Prison Theatre 17
   2.2. Grounding our Work 21

CHAPTER 3
Freedom from Within 27
   3.1. Escaping the Venue 27
   3.2. Breaking the Scene 32

CHAPTER 4
The Ensemble 39
   4.1. Connecting Inside 39
   4.2. Community Connection 47
   4.3. Connecting Outside 54

CHAPTER 5
Character Development 61
   5.1. Overcoming Challenges 61
   5.2. Unlocking Capacities 67

CHAPTER 6
Revising the Script 71
   6.1. Changing the Monologue 71
   6.2. Performing Agency 77

CHAPTER 7
Curtain Call 83

Appendix A
Literature 87

Appendix B
WHoS Productions and Projects 95

Appendix C
Methodological Considerations 99

References 111

List of Figures

Figure 3.1.	Bollywood dance in *Time Waits for No One* (2014 production)..	32
Figure 4.1.	The men working together to create visual effects in *Antigone* (2017 production)...	47
Figure 4.2.	Artist performing alongside the men in *Sleeping Giants* (2016 production)..............................	53
Figure 4.3.	Physical theatre performed in-the-round for *Chalk* (2010 production)..	59
Figure 5.1.	Singing and performing live music in *The Crossroads* (2018 production)	66
Figure 6.1.	The men performing as a part of *Here: A Captive Odyssey* (2015 production)........................	77
Figure 6.2.	The men on stage in *The Crossroads* (2018 production)...	82

List of Tables

Table 1.1.   Incarcerated WHoS Participants (n=15) 7

Table 1.2.   Former WHoS Participants (n=6) 9

Foreword

Kate Rubin and Jeni Luther

How do you get a group of twenty-seven incarcerated men, all strangers, to trust you, and to trust each other? For starters, you show up.

We sit down on the prison's couches and stare at the concrete walls, waiting for the men to arrive in the room, tucked in the Programs Building. Some stride in confidently, smiling. Some hover at the door waiting to be noticed. Some are quiet, and some seem to take up all the space in the room. A few arrive late.

The men's reactions mirror our own entrances. We are also entering an unknown place and walking into a culture we know very little about and can never fully understand. For them, stepping through the door is a big step out of their comfort zone and out of all they have known while incarcerated. For us, the encounter forces us to reach deeply into our knowledge and skills, struggling to kickstart a creative process in a restrictive environment.

Who are we? We are a collective of outside artists—performers, directors, set and lighting designers, stage technicians, videographers, puppeteers—who are passionate about art in prison. We are part of the woven fabric of William Head on Stage (WHoS). The reflections shared here are based on our own experiences, as well as those of outside artists who have worked with the men at William Head Institution over the past seventeen years. But artists of one kind or another have been interacting with the men of WHoS for the last forty-plus years, since it first started.

Many of us are self-employed artists. All of us share a passion to create theatre with those who are incarcerated and who may have never thought of themselves as artists. Many reasons draw us here to William Head Institution and to the WHoS space. We like the non-judgmental vulnerability that is in the room. We like to apply theatre to non-theatre settings. We like to co-create a space for artistic expression through a social justice lens. Working in this environment gives us the opportunity to support each other in a communal creative setting and gives us a chance to connect through teaching and collaboration.

Forty-four years ago, the men of William Head had a dream and a desire to participate in the arts. After taking a theatre course at the prison offered through the University of Victoria, the men started their own theatre company, which over the years blossomed into WHoS. They began by building connections with outside artists in Victoria, bringing them into the prison to direct and perform with them in their plays.

Since that time, WHoS has changed. Audiences have grown. The way in which the men produce, organize, and co-create with the outside artists has evolved. What started as a seed has developed into a beautiful (if delicate) flower that continues to be fed, watered, and nurtured by a new crop of inside and outside participants, all the while supported by the administration and staff of William Head Institution.

WHoS is theatre, but theatre of many kinds, from scripted plays, to devised theatre, and more recently through the ridiculous creativity of the COVID-19 pandemic, which saw us expand to films and podcasts. We found ways to compensate for the lack of actual audiences by producing online creative art exchanges, sharing creativity even when we could not share physical space.

We have been inspired by each other and by the expanding creativity and beautiful bravery of the men in the productions. The by-products of showing up and creating an inclusive space where anyone is welcome are tangible. We discover a place where the worry about not being creative can be shared. Brought out into the light, the sting of fear fades to shadows.

Once we are in the room with the men, we start with a sharing circle. A quick "touch base," giving each person a moment to enter the space. We stand up, we lead a stretch, we play a silly game, triggering laughter and revealing the connection, the release, in shared humour. Laughter can be fearful, dividing, but this laughter binds us together. As much as possible, we lead by doing. If you are going to ask people to quack like a duck, you have to quack like a duck yourself. When they realize that you are going to walk with them and not just tell them where to go, trust builds. Instead of the isolating platitude of "It's going to be okay," we say, "We will find a way through this together."

When we start the process of building a show, we all participate in creating the shape of the shared WHoS space. On a flipchart is a big piece of paper where we record how we will build a respectful working environment. Phrases appear on it, including thoughts like "Be on time," and "Leave your drama at the door." As a guideline, we always include "Trust the process" because once trust in the process begins, the door of curiosity opens. This is where we start asking, "What's next?," and we begin to listen, really listen, to each other's ideas. When that happens, we find the strength to take the risks of sharing a piece of writing, of standing up for a bit of improv, of singing a song, or of performing a dramatic monologue.

This is when the creative process takes off, reminding us of a key component—patience. Patience to meet people where they are at, patience to find ways of releasing preconceived notions, whether the expectations are about each other or about how the project is unfolding. Letting go of fears is hard enough, but letting go of hopes is even harder. We use creative problem solving, asking questions such as "What do our ideas have in common? ("What if there were gangs in the world of Oz?"); "What are unique suggestions we can all agree on?" ("Bollywood dance number, anyone?"); "Who can help with solutions?" ("Let's make a tornado out of a furnace fan! Can we make a giant sea serpent out of hula hoops and Christmas lights? How can we make a fake indoor campfire?"). Suddenly we find the happy, chaotic freedom that we need to create a (sometimes strange and loopy) plan for what we want to do.

When a major part of the planning is done, the work of devising play material, set building, and rehearsal begins. This is when hidden gems start to appear at WHoS. One of our jobs as artists is to see those little jewels, know them for what they are, and bring them into the light. The shared experiences of overcoming stage fright, learning lines (and forgetting lines), sewing costumes, making props, designing lighting and sound, learning stage management duties, marketing the shows (including handling the WHoS budgets!) brings the cast and crew together as a working team.

WHoS is therefore a collective project, one where the men choose to come, choose to commit, and choose to band together to create a production. Performing the shows for a live audience is the icing on the cake, as it means those on the outside get to enter the prison gates and come into the gymnasium to see a WHoS performance. For most of the men it is their first time performing and for many, the first time interacting with the public.

An essential part of WHoS is the recognition and appreciation that the cast and crew receive for their hard work. This comes in the form of smiles and standing ovations from the audience at the end of the show, written comments received, and the question-and-answer period, where the public has an opportunity to acknowledge and validate the team's efforts.

WHoS is a unique society created by and for incarcerated men. As outside artists we feel grateful to be a part of it. We are thankful for the privilege of trust. We cherish the experiences of nurturing curiosity, bravely letting go, and finding a supportive space where we can be reminded of the power of creativity and theatre-making and learn to trust the process.

Ridha and Frigon's *Staging Prison Theatre in Canada: Setting the Spotlight on William Head on Stage* is an illuminating book that tells the story of WHoS through the voices of the men involved. By examining the impact of this unique theatre initiative, they offer an insightful and academic perspective on the power of prison theatre. The book provides new avenues of appreciation for the work of WHoS and is an essential read for artists, criminologists, correctional personnel, and anyone interested in the transformative nature of theatre.

Acknowledgements

We would like to acknowledge and recognize all the men who have participated in William Head on Stage (WHoS). Thank you for your combined efforts that have allowed this initiative to blossom and grow. To the men who took part in this study, to you we extend our utmost gratitude and appreciation. Thank you for opening your hearts, sharing your experiences, and letting us be a part of the WHoS family. We hope your words resonate throughout this book.

A sincere thanks and appreciation to the community artists and volunteers of WHoS. May you continue to artistically create and inspire all those around you. To the staff at Correctional Service Canada and William Head Institution, thank you for embracing this research. A special thank you to William Head Institution's Management Services and Program staff for their unbounded support.

We extend our thanks to the University of Ottawa Press and staff who helped us bring this book to life. Importantly, this journey would not be possible without the ongoing encouragement, support, and patience of our family.

We would like to gratefully acknowledge the financial support received from the Social Sciences and Humanities Research Council of Canada and the Collabzium "Always Be Closing" Grant from the Faculty of Social Sciences, University of Ottawa.

CHAPTER 1

The Opening Script

> WHoS is special [...] Having the opportunity and the feeling of building something—especially through art—it's unique; I don't think you're going to get that anywhere else.
>
> – Sammy, incarcerated WHoS participant

Tucked into the deep forests of Metchosin, British Columbia, William Head Institution sits at the southern tip of Vancouver Island. Enclosed on three sides by the waves of the Pacific Ocean, this minimum-security prison for men is home to William Head on Stage (WHoS), Canada's only prison theatre run by inmates, which has been operating for over forty years. Every year, in the fall, the men of WHoS invite the public for the exclusive opportunity to enter the prison walls and experience their captivating theatre production. While the magic of WHoS and the alluring work of the men have been the subject of media stories over the years, the research and academic literature on WHoS is largely absent.

Indeed, the development of the research in this book came about through reading news articles on WHoS, in which descriptions of the productions and the involvement of the men, at every stage of the theatrical process, raised more questions than answers—a theatre initiative, happening in a prison, running for decades, here in Canada?

Thana Ridha's criminological background combined with her appreciation of the arts drew her into wanting to explore the nuances of WHoS and seek to understand the experiences of the men involved with this theatre initiative. Having carried out research both academically and professionally, largely through quantitative approaches in criminology, Thana was eager to engage in more creative research looking at WHoS and prison theatre more broadly. We were matching puzzle pieces, because as a criminologist, Sylvie Frigon focuses much of her research looking at the arts in prison, including dance and literature within spaces of confinement. When we first met to discuss the possibility of conducting research looking at WHoS, we quickly realized that this would not only be research that we are interested and passionate about, but one that is warranted to highlight the work of WHoS.

While across the globe, numerous countries including Brazil, the United Kingdom, New Zealand, the United States, and Lebanon operate arts-based initiatives in prison, such as theatre, the research examining such artistic initiatives remains largely underdeveloped (Hughes 2005; McAvinchey 2020; Tocci 2007). Criminological research and correctional research have predominately focused on examining structured interventions in prison that are rehabilitative and aim to directly address risk factors associated with offending, such as correctional programs (Andrews 1989; Andrews and Bonta 2010). Given this, prison theatre and other arts-based initiatives have largely been left in the shadows of research. To help merge the gap in the literature between the arts and criminology while expanding the research on prison theatre, this book serves as a case study on WHoS. Given the limited understandings around prison theatre within the criminological literature and considering the absence of such research in Canada, despite the long-standing operation of WHoS, our exploratory case study seeks to unpack the experiences of the men with WHoS. As such, to frame this major research area, we sought to acknowledge the experiences of the participants with WHoS, as well as understand how this prison theatre initiative fits into the broader prison context in Canada.

To address these questions and expand the current state of knowledge on the impacts of prison theatre, we were interested in hearing directly from personal experiences and testimonies of men who have taken part in WHoS, while also observing the magic that takes place at WHoS. To accomplish this, we conducted site visits to WHoS at William Head Institution and qualitative interviews with incarcerated WHoS participants and formerly incarcerated WHoS participants in the community. Through this approach, our study aims to develop in-depth understandings that foreground the experiences of the men as criminalized individuals; a population whose voices are widely overlooked in both the literature on prison theatre and the criminological research more broadly (Brown 2008; Ricciardelli 2014a; Schlosser 2008). These men embraced our presence and interest in WHoS, and with notable candour, shared their experiences with us. By including both incarcerated as well as formally incarcerated WHoS participants, we sought to develop holistic and nuanced understandings of the men's experiences by capturing both the short-term and long-term impacts of their involvement with WHoS.

With much of the emerging discourses around prison theatre stemming from the discipline of applied theatre, the literature has yet to thoroughly engage or consider the prison backdrop in which prison theatre initiatives operate.[1] That is, much of the research has been descriptive, done by theatre practitioners and artists reflecting on their own practice or observations within prison theatre. As criminologists, we adopt a unique new lens and approach that involves the testimonies of the participants themselves as well as analyses that consider prison theatre engagement within the context of prison, imprisonment, and confinement more broadly. By integrating a conceptual framework that captures both the structural and social systems of prison, this book unpacks how the impact of prison theatre may be shaped and conceptualized in the prison context.

1.1. Narrating the WHoS Story

Over the course of its long-standing operation, WHoS has produced more than fifty-six theatre productions.[2] Each year, WHoS opens close to fourteen shows whereby the public has the exclusive and unique opportunity to purchase tickets, come into the prison, and experience the captivating performances. While in some years these productions are based on the reimagining of existing plays or novels, in other years the productions represent originally devised material. In 2015, WHoS put together a production on the history of William Head Institution as a quarantine station, using theatre, shadow art, puppetry, and live music to have the audience travel back in time. In 2018, WHoS reimagined Sophocles' tragedy *Antigone* into a science-fiction rendition with restorative justice elements. Over the years, WHoS has orchestrated a range of productions that are unique in their own way and incorporate the diverse backgrounds, experiences, and cultures of the men

---

[1] Appendix A provides a brief overview of the literature on prison theatre.
[2] Appendix B lists all WHoS productions and projects over the years.

involved. Having attended various productions over the years, we find that WHoS never fails to mesmerize the audience with their performances and degree of professionalism. Each year, the gymnasium of the institution transforms into a theatre space, complete with a set, stage, and a floor filled with seats for the audience.

As an inmate-run initiative, WHoS functions as a not-for-profit society and theatre company that the men themselves operate (WHoS, n.d). Operating uniquely in this way, the men of WHoS are involved in all the facets associated with the company's functioning and creative processes. This includes taking on the role of actors, costume designers, set builders and designers, and even writers. In turn, the men's involvement with WHoS is both multifaceted and a collaborative process. With an array of duties associated with putting on a production, being a part of WHoS is voluntary and is open to all prisoners within the institution who are interested in participating. Every year, WHoS donates a portion of the ticket revenue to a selected charitable organization, while most funds go towards supporting the following year's theatre production.

In or around March each year, WHoS commences the planning, designing, and preparation of its yearly fall production, which opens to the public in October. WHoS works alongside a group of dedicated volunteer artists from the community who help support and mentor the men with the theatre devising and production process. The artists are actively involved in assisting WHoS in various aspects related to music, lighting, and set design, while also assisting with the facilitation of workshops. These workshops, which occur in preparation for the production, take place several days each month and involve a range of theatre activities, such as improvisational games and coaching the men on acting. In addition to providing artistic support and mentorship, the volunteer artists may also perform in WHoS productions alongside the men. With regards to the production, each year WHoS hires a theatre director over the summer that collaborates with the men and helps in orchestrating the production. The director works closely alongside the men of WHoS to devise scripts, facilitate role rehearsals, and guide the overall theatre process. Further to the volunteer and community support, WHoS also has a board of directors consisting of participating prisoners who are responsible for the various organizational aspects of the theatre company. Among its many responsibilities, the WHoS board of directors takes care of any administrative features, marketing aspects, as well as any negotiations required with the administrative staff at the institution. All WHoS activities take place in the Programs Building of William Head Institution, which also houses the gymnasium where the annual WHoS productions take place.

Operating within a prison, having members of the public come into William Head Institution requires extensive security protocols to support this undertaking. These security measures include electronic scanning and the use of detector dogs. As a part of the procedures, audience members must be over the age of nineteen and all items and personal belongings are restricted for entry into the institution. Evidently, weeks of planning and collaboration occur with the institution's administration, to ensure appropriate staff presence and security measures are arranged. However, having been in operation for over four decades and entrenched within the history of the prison, the administration and management at William Head Institution are well equipped to support WHoS and make the productions possible. Despite WHoS being an inmate-run initiative, given the prison context it operates in, the administration of William Head Institution oversees the operation of WHoS. Notably, the Social Program Officer is the coordinating liaison for WHoS and supports the men in their communication with the institution, community artists, and volunteers. The Social Program Officer further helps facilitate any material and equipment purchasing, as well as the scheduling of events and activities related to WHoS.

WHoS operates in the Correctional Service Canada (CSC) under social programs and leisure activities. As per CSC's Commissioner's Directive 760, leisure activities are, "structured and unstructured activities that encourage inmates to develop and maintain a healthy, pro-social lifestyle and to use their time constructively" (2016). In this regard, WHoS workshops and performances all generally take place at times outside of the men's scheduled working hours or structured programs. While operating as a leisure activity, the development of WHoS traces back to the post-secondary education program offered in federal institutions across British Columbia in the 1970s (Duguid 1998). In partnership with the University of Victoria and Simon Fraser University, inmates were able to earn course credits by taking part in various university courses related to humanities, social sciences, and theatre. In 1975, following the two-year operation of the post-secondary education program, inmates in Matsqui Institution organized a prison theatre group called the Institutional

Theatre Productions (Prihar and Little 2014). This inmate-run theatre group ran for six years at Matsqui Institution until 1981, during which a prison riot led to the halt of the initiative. During this year, many inmates from Matsqui Institution were transferred to William Head Institution, including many of whom were involved in the prison theatre initiative (Prihar and Little 2014). In turn, in 1981, prison theatre found a new beginning at William Head Institution under the name William Head Amateur Theatre (WHAT), in association with the post-secondary education program offered through the University of Victoria. While the post-secondary education program at William Head Institution ended in 1984, with the support of volunteer artists and institutional staff the prison theatre initiative was continued by the men and operates to this day as WHoS.

1.2. Narrating the Experiences with WHoS

To obtain a better understanding of the impact of theatre on the lives of criminalized individuals from their personal perspective and experiences, we conducted qualitative, individual, semi-structured interviews with fifteen current WHoS participants and six former WHoS participants. Conducting interviews was most suitable as it is a method of inquiry that is not detached or disconnected from the men. In turn, conducting interviews allowed understandings to form from the direct testimony of individuals who either are, or have been, involved with WHoS (Alasuutari 1995). The interview and data-collection process took place in October of 2017, during the WHoS production of *Antigone*. Appendix C details the methodology employed, including the research and data collection processes, analysis, as well as ethical considerations.

The participants interviewed can be divided into two main groups. The first group includes incarcerated WHoS participants (current prisoners) while the second group includes former WHoS participants who are no longer incarcerated (former prisoners).[3] Given that WHoS operates at a federal institution, all the men in our study either are serving or have served a federal sentence of two years or more.

---

3   To protect the identities of the participants, all names have been replaced with pseudonyms.

1.2.1. Incarcerated WHoS Participants

This group comprises of fifteen men incarcerated at William Head Institution who have participated in WHoS. We were interested in hearing from any of the men who have experience being a part of WHoS in any capacity, to allow for diversified experiences to be captured in this research. In turn, this group of participants includes individuals who have been involved in various WHoS productions and with different roles. Though each participant interviewed has taken on the role of an actor in at least one WHoS production, many of the participants have other levels of experience in the company, including but not limited to being: board members, assistant stage managers, costume designers, musicians, painters, set designers, and numerous other behind-the-scenes involvements. Of the fifteen incarcerated WHoS participants, six have been involved with WHoS for one production while nine have participated in the theatre company for several productions.

Table 1.1. Incarcerated WHoS Participants (n=15)

Participant	
Brandon	Brandon has acted in two WHoS productions and has also taken part in costume design.
Rick	Rick has been involved with WHoS for over four years and has both acted and played in the band for WHoS.
Thomas	Thomas is participating in WHoS for his first time and is taking on the role of an actor while also assisting with costume and set design.
Karl	Karl has been involved in WHoS in various ways over the course of his five-year participation, ranging from acting, set design, and make-up.
Joe	Joe has been involved in WHoS for four years and has taken on various acting roles, played as a musician in the band, and has been involved in costume making.
Samuel	Samuel has been a part of WHoS for five years, taking on various roles such as actor, musician, board member as well as sound/music technician.
Jackson	Jackson is participating in WHoS for the first time as an actor while also assisting with set design.

Participant	
Jayden	Jayden is taking part in WHoS for the first year as an actor in the production.
Michael	Michael has participated in WHoS for over five years and has taken on various acting positions and has been involved in costume design.
Dave	Dave has been a part of WHoS for two years where he has been involved as both an actor and WHoS board member.
Sammy	Sammy has been a part of WHoS for three years and has taken on various acting positions.
Logan	Logan is participating with WHoS for his first time and is taking on the role of an actor while also assisting with costumes.
Kevin	Kevin has been involved with WHoS over the course of seven years in various roles including actor and assistant stage manager.
Andre	Andre is participating in his first year with WHoS as an actor.
Zane	Zane is participating in WHoS for first time and is taking on an acting role.

1.2.2. Former WHoS Participants

This group includes six men who are no longer incarcerated but have participated in WHoS prior to their release from prison. Similarly to the first group, these individuals have also been involved in WHoS in different capacities and over the course of various years. Of the six men who were interviewed, five had been involved with WHoS for more than one year. While all the former WHoS participants have taken on acting roles in WHoS, many of them have been entrenched in other aspects of the company throughout their years of involvement where they took on roles such as board members, assistant stage managers, costume designers, musicians, painters, set designers, and even writers. Of these former WHoS participants, three of the men disclosed that they were released from prison within the past year while the remaining three have been in the community for several years.

Table 1.2. Former WHoS Participants (*n*=6)

Participant	
Seth	Seth was involved with WHoS for five years and participated in different aspects of the theatre company including acting, assisting with the administration, as well as taking part in set design and props.
Jake	Jake was involved in WHoS for ten years where he participated in various capacities, taking on roles such as set designer, carpenter, actor, as well as assisting with the administration aspects of the production.
Armin	Armin participated in WHoS for one year where he was involved as an actor in the production.
Lincoln	Lincoln was a part of WHoS for five years and took on several roles in the theatre company where he participated as an actor, producer, and stage manager, as well as assisted in various administrative and organizational aspects of WHoS.
Dylan	Dylan took part in WHoS for two years where he produced music for the productions as well as took part in acting.
Andrew	Andrew was involved in WHoS for about thirteen years where he was involved as an actor, assistant, writer, board member, in addition to taking part in various other administrative aspects of the company.

1.3. Positionality

Parallel to the integrative nature of prison theatre that unites the arts with prison, we situate this research within the creative framework of imaginative criminology.[4] Criminology as a discipline has been dominated by quantitative research approaches characterized by an epistemology that is objectivist, and a methodology that is experimental (Guba and Lincoln 1994). Imaginative criminology as a quality of mind challenges this positivist, mainstream approach to criminological research. As Young (2011) asserts in his seminal work *The Criminological Imagination*, there appears to be an overreliance for numbers within the

---

4   First coined by Jock Young (2011) as the criminological imagination. Imaginative criminology as a quality of mind is an adaption of Mills's (1959) sociological imagination whereby he promotes a critical examination of the unquestioned state of scientific knowledge (Piamonte 2016).

discipline of criminology. However, quantitative research centred on quantifying, measuring, and evaluating runs the risk of being reductionist whereby the dimensions of experiences and complex phenomena are ultimately, "[…] lost in a sea of statistical symbols and dubious analysis" (Young 2011, viii).

In line with the vision of imaginative criminology, we too perceive the need to broaden mainstream approaches in criminological thought. With the aim of developing in-depth understandings of the impact of prison theatre on the lives of criminalized individuals from the experiences of the participants, it was essential to adopt a qualitative approach (Attride-Stirling 2001; Hammersley 2013). As Jacobsen (2014, 3) describes, "quantitative methods may show the scope and range of a given phenomenon […] however, [they] are not appropriate when seeking to understand a phenomenon creatively from the 'inside,' as it were, considering the humanistic coefficient." That is, quantitative approaches may be able to capture the recidivism and reoffending rates of prison theatre participants, though such approaches ultimately offer limited understandings given the disconnect from the participants. By attending to the voices of the men involved with WHoS, unconfined to statistical measures, tools, and variables, more expansive and comprehensive understandings can be made regarding the experiences and impacts of the prison theatre.

While imaginative criminology calls for the break away from the iron cage of positivism when it comes to doing research, a similar call is found within the applied theatre literature.[5] Introduced by Thompson (2009), the affective turn is the rejection of the evaluation discourse around applied theatre whereby the focus is on measuring and quantifying impacts of artistic initiatives (Khutan 2014). In his discussion on the affective turn, Thompson (2009) calls for the examination of applied theatre practices, such as prison theatre, in terms of their aesthetic merit and affect.[6] At its base, the affective turn in applied theatre denounces the overreliance given to quantitative approaches for studying the arts whereby the emphasis has been on evaluation through statistical

---

5   A term coined by Max Weber in 1905 to represent the increased rationalization in society that traps individuals in systems of teleological efficiency and rational calculation.

6   Thompson (2009) refers to *affect* as the embodied response provoked by aesthetic experience or otherwise the emotional, sensory, and aesthetic side of theatre. In his book *Performance Affects*, Thompson (2009) offers a full, detailed discussion on the affective turn.

outcomes and measures (Thompson 2009). A qualitative approach for examining WHoS is not only more conductive of developing in-depth understandings, but, in part, it responds to the calls found within both the criminological and applied theatre literature.

Further to this, engaging with imaginative criminology offers a means of expanding the criminological milieu into one where the creative arts, such as theatre, may be recognized as meaningful areas of inquiry within the field. In adopting an imaginative lens and approach, we view the examination of arts-based theatre initiatives in prison as a significant area of inquiry for criminology. Criminological research encompassing creative topics or arts-based approaches are often regarded as unconventional to the field. That is, through this book, we aim to shed light into how arts-based initiatives fit into the prison setting and more specifically how they can operate as positive tools in the lives of criminalized individuals. Mainstream criminological research tends to focus primarily on interventions in prison that are guided by a rehabilitative and correctional agenda, such as correctional programs that target risk factors directly linked to offending (Andrews 1989; Andrews and Bonta 2010; Duriez et al. 2018). As such, little attention has been given to other programs and services that are available in prison, or what Siganos (2008) refers to as cultural activities, which may further support successful reintegration. On a more basic level, prison theatre can be seen as a non-traditional criminological object of investigation as it represents an initiative that transgresses the boundaries of conventional practices and initiatives typically found inside prison.

As Seal and O'Neil (2021) note, imaginative criminology explores spaces of transgression and pays attention to how these spaces come to be experienced as sites of resistance. Building on this, Branders (2018; 2020; 2023) introduces a unique focus of looking at the subversive effects of prison theatre. Through her extensive research and field work on theatre in Belgian prisons, Branders's (2023) examination entails the conceptualization of theatre as a subversive activity or space within the prison setting. Subversion may be regarded as serving an activist project in criminology as it encapsulates the undermining or overthrow of established orders or systems, such as prisons. For Branders (2023), the very act of organizing and doing theatre in prison is not a neutral one, but one that is paradoxical to the norms and constraints typically observed. Art and theatre offer experiences and potential that other activities within prison do not, such as allowing for freedom of expression, imagination, and play. As such, rather than focusing on prison theatre's effect through quasi-scientific rhetoric, Branders (2023) theoretically highlights how, in staging theatre, subversion can be creatively played out within the prison.

We are inspired by these insights of imaginative criminology that move away from positivism and quantitative approaches, all of which influence mainstream criminological understanding and to which criminologists routinely subscribe. As envisioned by Frauley (2015) in his work *On Imaginative Criminology and Its Significance*, imaginative criminology breaks away from positions and assumptions that are doxic. Drawing on Bourdieu and Eagleton's (1992) seminal development, doxa refers to the taken-for-granted understandings that are unquestionable and seen as common-sense, or otherwise natural (Frauley 2015). In this work, we aim to expand the purview of criminology to further encompass arts-based approaches and initiatives. Doing this can help contribute to the resonating call within the literature to alter or break away from the conventional and dominant positivist approaches that dominate the field (Frauley 2015; Jacobsen 2014; Seal and O'Neil 2021).

Unlocking imagination in criminological research is not done through a specific key, nor is there a definitive requirement of what constitutes imaginative criminology (Carlen 2016). Indeed, if this were the case, imaginative criminology would, ironically, be rather unimaginative. Instead, imaginative criminology is an overarching lens or framework that challenges mainstream criminological conventions, approaches, and even methodologies. This may precisely be done through the selection and examination of unconventional criminological objects, such as theatre, which transgress either the disciplinary boundary or the boundary of conventional practice (Frauley 2015). For example, the transgression of disciplinary boundaries of imaginative criminology is exemplified by the creative work of Frigon (2014; 2015; 2019) on dance in prisons. In her research, Frigon (2014; 2015; 2019) offers a new way of understanding women's experiences of imprisonment through the medium of dance and choreographic performances.

As Jacobsen (2014, 14) notes in his call to reimagine a criminology that is more creatively oriented, "all sciences may indeed benefit—every now and then—from deploying a more playful and imaginative attitude towards their studies and research procedures." While theatre may appear to be futile from a mainstream criminological perspective, exploring the experiences of the men with WHoS and considering the impact it has on their lives can help shed unique insight to both the research on prison theatre and criminological research more broadly. Our approach can thus be seen as the theoretical crossroads that joins criminology with the theatrical arts.

Further to the framework that we adopt here, Brown (1996, 19) describes how, "Investigators must step into their own spotlight and with a cold eye, and assess their behaviour and thoughts [...]". Reflexivity, as a strategy, allows for researchers to be mindful or conscious of their own role in the research process (Hesse-Biber and Leavy 2006; Grbich 2004; Mortari 2015). Since embarking on this project, we have attempted to engage in reflexive practice by continuously reflecting on our position as criminologists and researchers, as well as on the interplay of discourses that not only shape us, but inevitably also influence our approach to this research (Grbich 2004; Hammersley and Atkinson 1983). In line with Grbich's (2004) discussion on the role of researchers, we do not position ourselves in the hierarchal role of "experts." Instead, we regard ourselves as learners, in that it is through the experiences shared by the participants that we want to understand the impacts of theatre (Berg and Lune 2006).

In conducting our research, the concept of voice was regarded as central to this study as we are principally attending to the experiences of the participants in order to gain an understanding of the impact of theatre on the lives of criminalized individuals (Guba and Lincoln 1994). As criminologists we are deeply aware of how the voices, perspectives, and experiences of criminalized individuals are latent and often overlooked in research. This is particularly the case for incarcerated individuals as access to this population is fundamentally limited and restricted (Ricciardelli 2014a; Schlosser 2008). The academic literature on prison theatre is no exception to this. With the recognition that agency or voice cannot inherently be taken away or given to individuals, our aim in this book is not to fundamentally "give" voice to the participants (Ezzy 2002). Instead, this book serves as a means for allowing the voices of criminalized individuals to be heard. Therefore, an underlying premise of our study is to bring the experiences of criminalized individuals to the front stage of criminological research. While the research may be understood as a co-creation of knowledge between the participants and ourselves, we attempt to foreground the voices of the participants and present them as authentically as possible throughout the book (HesseBiber and Leavy 2006).

1.4. Organization of the Book

Before beginning the examination of the men's experiences with WHoS, Chapter 2, "Setting the Stage", engages with broader discussions on prison theatre. We illustrate a conceptualization of prison theatre and consider the dominant discourses underlying the approaches that shape these initiatives. The following part of this chapter foregrounds the theoretical underpinnings we adopt in subsequent chapters for analyzing the narratives of the men. Discussions are framed by criminological theorizations on imprisonment, namely Goffman's (1961) total institutions, as well as the structural and social context of prison. We turn to conceptual developments around the social structures of prison as they relate to the inmate culture (Clemmer 1940) and prison masculinities (Ricciardelli 2015) to further understand and anchor the experiences of the men with WHoS.

Chapter 3, "Freedom from Within", looks at the confinement associated with imprisonment and the freedom associated with theatre. Through the examination of the men's experiences with WHoS and the application of relevant theorization on imprisonment, this chapter unravels how WHoS represents an alternative space within the prison context and a form of escapism for the men. Building on the discussion of space, the second part of the chapter highlights the emotional awareness and expression that WHoS fosters. Through the incorporation of theoretical understandings around the emotional geography of prison, we uncover how WHoS represents an intermission to the normative emotional scene. Discussion centres on the distinct space WHoS offers and the various ways the men experience emotional growth through their involvement with WHoS.

Chapter 4, "The Ensemble", is comprised of three parts that highlight the capacity of WHoS to build community both within the prison and on the outside. Through the application of conceptual understandings around the prison social system and inmate culture, the first section reveals the unique camaraderie and collaboration WHoS fosters amongst the men. The second section explores the unique significance of the connections made at WHoS with the volunteers and artists from the community. The third part discusses the community engagement aspect of WHoS by looking at how the theatre company may be understood as an avenue for the participating inmates to connect and communicate with the "outside." Through the presentation and analysis of the men's narratives, this chapter argues how public perceptions and (mis)understandings around prisoners or incarceration may come to be renegotiated through WHoS.

Chapter 5, "Character Development", will unearth how the men step out of their comfort zones and overcome personal challenges through their engagement with WHoS. By stretching themselves beyond their habituated engagements and experiences within prison, discussions will explore how WHoS helps unlock the participants' capacities, skills, and confidence in themselves. Following this, Chapter 6, "Revising the Script", pertains to the men's narratives around themselves. As will be analyzed through the narratives, in the prison context where the sense of self is constantly contested, WHoS becomes instrumental in building the participants' self-esteem and self-worth. Additionally, we shed light on how the men are able to perform their agency, or otherwise assert their independence through their involvement with WHoS. We draw from Goffman's (1961) theorization of total institutions, which capture the limitations and restrictions associated with incarceration to understand how the inmate-run composition of WHoS contrasts with the structural context of prison whereby personal autonomy and independence are often compromised. In the conclusion, Chapter 7, "Curtain Call", we weave together the strands of analyses and men's narratives to substantiate the significance of WHoS. We set out the contributions of this research and how it anchors the relevance of operating arts-based initiatives in prison.

CHAPTER 2

Setting the Stage

This chapter provides an overview of the discourses around prison theatre. The first section introduces the discussion on the conceptualization of prison theatre. This includes outlining current understandings around these initiatives. Following this, we look briefly at the different approaches that shape these initiatives. Importantly, we foreground the reader with some of the main theoretical underpinnings we adopt in our analyses.

2.1. Approaches to Prison Theatre

The application or use of theatre can be seen in a variety of contexts, from educational settings in schools to institutional settings in prisons. Prison theatre as a practice can be best understood as stemming from the discipline of applied theatre, which involves the application of theatre in community settings or with marginalized populations (Nicholson 2014). Over the years, there has been a cultivating interest in the application of arts-based initiatives, such as theatre, with criminalized populations and in prison settings. The discursive shift in criminological research from "nothing works" (Martinson 1974) with regards to the rehabilitation and reintegration of prisoners to "what works" may have helped propagate the development of these arts-based programs (Day 2013; McGuire 1995). While the literature around prison theatre only began to emerge in recent decades, prison theatre as a practice has been around for centuries.

Although the development of prison theatre does not have a clearly documented history, there have been notable initiatives or "significant moments" that may be associated with the advancement of prison theatre (McAvinchy 2020; Thompson 1998, 6). In his book *The Proscenium Cage*, Tocci (2007) notes that theatre practices for prisoners have been around since the 1890s. Other scholars and theatre practitioners, such as

McAvinchey (2011), established that prison theatre goes as far back as 1789, when prisoners in the colony of New South Wales staged dramatist George Farquhar's work *The Recruiting Officer* (McAvinchey 2011).[1] In the 1950s, the San Quentin Drama Workshop was founded in San Quentin State Prison as one of the first prison theatre initiatives in the United States (McAvinchey 2011; Tocci 2007). However, it was not until the 1960s and 1970s that prison theatre began to achieve a significant presence globally (Tocci 2007), with prison theatre in Canada also beginning during this time, through the prison post-secondary education program in British Columbia (Duguid 1998). Since then, many countries across the globe have been operating theatre initiatives for criminalized populations.

Considering the many initiatives and programs around the world, prison theatre is not a homogenous practice. That is, diversity exists in what prison theatre is and can be. While some initiatives involve the participating prisoners working with notable literary work, such as Shakespeare, others focus on devising and creating original plays. Similarly, some prison theatre initiatives centre on the development of a production, with participants involved in the various aspects of theatre-making, such as set design and costumes, others place greater emphasis on working with theatre techniques and practices. Notably, as Lucas (2021) indicates in her work examining prison theatre across the globe, the manifestation of a prison theatre, with regards to what it can or cannot be, is largely determined by the prison administration. This in turn also points to the diversity we see in prison theatre as a practice, with each initiative shaped by the mould of the prison's administration and security requirements in terms of what can be done or supported. Notwithstanding the different ways prison theatre may operate, these initiatives appear to often be constructed around one of two general dominant discourses: theatre as drama therapy, and theatre as education or rehabilitation.

2.1.1. Theatre as Drama Therapy

Drama therapy is founded on the healing characteristics that are present in the creative processes of drama and theatre activities (Langley

---

[1] These were prisoners of the First Fleet, comprised of ships that transported convicts from Great Britain to Australia. At this time, several penal colonies were established in different parts of Australia, which served to detain individuals away from civilian settlements.

2006; Leeder and Wimmer 2007). The North American Drama Therapy Association defines drama therapy as, "the intentional use of drama and/or theatre processes to achieve therapeutic goals" (n.d.). Rooted in both psychotherapy and theatre, the interactive and creative processes used in drama therapy allow individuals to express their emotions and feelings while developing interpersonal skills. While drama was used alongside mainstream therapeutic practices in the beginning of the twentieth century, by the 1930s, drama therapy began to emerge as its own discipline (Jones 2007). Within this framework, theatre and drama are understood as being therapeutic mediums capable of facilitating healing and personal change (Landy 1996; Langley 2006). That is, theatre techniques and practices are used to work through behaviour and attitudes through a therapeutic lens. Drama therapy has fluidity as it may involve different theatrical techniques such as storytelling, projective play, improvisation, movement, and even performance. Often led by drama therapists or theatre practitioners, drama therapy in prison settings can be practised in either individual or group settings. A key aspect of drama therapy is that individuals can engage with themselves and their personal challenges through these practices (Baim et al. 2002; Jones 2007; Landy 1996). Drama therapy approaches to prison theatre partly involve allowing individuals to make self-reflections, such as connections between childhood and offending behaviour (Landy 1996). The Geese Theatre Company is a prison theatre initiative that stems largely from this approach. Adopted from the original Geese Theatre Program in the United States, this company, established in the United Kingdom in 1987, operates interactive drama-based workshops and group activities within the criminal justice system. Though the Geese Theatre Company is not strictly a drama therapy program, it recognizes the therapeutic potential of drama and thus encompasses elements of drama therapy techniques (Baim et al. 2002; Thompson 1998). While drama therapy is one method used in prison theatre practices, the vast majority of theatre initiatives fall under the approach of theatre as education or rehabilitation.

2.1.2. Theatre as Education or Rehabilitation

Theatre as education or rehabilitation is an approach whereby drama-based and theatrical techniques are used as an avenue for personal development (Moller 2003). Rather than being viewed as therapeutic sessions, prison theatre programs that subscribe to the educational and rehabilitative framework often operate workshops that focus on theatre-making and devising. Professional actors and directors, as well as volunteers, may take part in leading these workshops. This approach emphasizes collaboration and allowing prisoners to connect and work together as part of a group. In turn, prison theatre initiatives that correspond with this framework provide opportunities for prisoners to both learn and practise social skills (Bailin 1993). The role of participants in these prison theatre programs extends beyond acting, as individuals may be involved in different aspects of theatre and take on various roles (Moller 2013). The Rehabilitation Through the Arts program in the United States is illustrative of this approach, whereby engaging in theatre and the arts aids in the development of skills that are understood to be supportive of the rehabilitation and reintegration process for those involved (Moller 2003). Rehabilitation Through the Arts has been operating since 1996 in prisons across the United States and offers a variety of arts-based programs, such as music, dance, and visual arts (Halperin et al. 2012).

Given the correctional realm in which prison theatre operates, it is not uncommon for arts-based initiatives to be framed by their rehabilitative value (Day 2019; Pensalfini 2019; Woodland and Hazou 2021). As Moyes (2019) describes through her role as a national arts in corrections adviser in New Zealand, art programs, such as prison theatre, should not be dismissed as merely "constructive activities," but rather recognized for their potential and integral role in supporting rehabilitation. While most theatre programs are mandated in education and rehabilitation, they nonetheless may incorporate techniques of drama therapy or have the capacity to provide therapeutic aspects for prisoners. That is, a program that is not operating within the framework of drama therapy may still have therapeutic elements to it. Likewise, programs that are framed by therapy may have educational and rehabilitative potentials. For example, despite aligning with the approach of drama therapy, the Geese Theatre Company can also be understood as engaging with a rehabilitation paradigm, as evidenced by the incorporation of drama-based techniques to motivate individual change (Balfour et al. 2019; Day 2019). In turn, while the discourses around the development of prison theatre programs are largely dominated by either therapeutic or educational/rehabilitative agendas, they are not to be viewed as conflicting or otherwise opposing approaches. Furthermore, while most prison theatre programs operate within the frameworks of therapy or education/rehabilitation, some initiatives, like WHoS, are not entirely guided by either approach.

WHoS may be seen as reminiscent of the theatre as education and rehabilitation framework, given that it arose from the post-secondary education program offered through the University of Victoria. However, following the closure of the education program at William Head Institution in 1984, WHoS has been operating independently as an inmate-run theatre company and not-for-profit society. As opposed to being mandated as an educational or rehabilitative program, WHoS is a theatre initiative that devises and produces performances for the public. Notwithstanding the uniqueness of WHoS, given the therapeutic and rehabilitative agendas that underpin many of the prison theatre initiatives around the world, discourses around these frameworks dominate the literature on prison theatre (Pensalfini 2016).

2.2. Grounding our Work

As we aim to understand and contextualize the experiences of the men with WHoS, we weave together theoretical understandings around both the structural and social context of prison. While we have aimed to make this book accessible to a wide audience by not overwhelming the reader with theoretically dense assertions, we nonetheless recognize that presenting some of the main theoretical understandings that form the conceptual framework of this work is essential. In this section we highlight the importance of using an integrative conceptual framework that draws on the prison backdrop against which prison theatre operates, and grounds the reader with a basis of the principal theoretical underpinnings we employ in our analysis.

Much of the emerging discourse around prison theatre stems from the discipline of applied theatre. In turn, to expand the literature, we apply a unique criminological approach that considers the prison context. By integrating a conceptual framework that captures both the structural and social systems of prison, this study unravels how the impact of prison theatre may be shaped and conceptualized against the prison context. We incorporate relevant conceptualizations around the structural and social setting of prison by merging early theoretical understandings on prison, such as that developed by Erving Goffman (1961) and Clemmer (1940), with more contemporary conceptual understandings on prison such as that of Crewe et al. (2014) and Ricciardelli (2014a; 2014b). By drawing on Goffman's

(1961) theorization of total institutions as well as conceptual developments around the social structures of prison as they relate to the inmate culture (Clemmer 1940) and prison masculinities (Ricciardelli 2015), we develop more nuanced understandings of the experiences of the men with WHoS.

Canadian-American sociologist Erving Goffman is known for his various influential works situated within the framework of symbolic interactionism.[2] Of particular relevance to this study, we turn to the theoretical developments Goffman presents in his seminal work *Asylums* whereby he introduces the conceptualization of total institutions, which he theorizes as:

> [...] A place of residence and work where a large number of like-situated individuals cut off from the wider society for an appreciable period of time together lead an enclosed formally administered round of life. (1961, xiii)

While Goffman (1961) develops his idea of the total institutions from his participant observational study of the St. Elizabeths Psychiatric Hospital in Washington, D.C, he extends it to other social establishments, such as the military, boarding schools, and of relevance to this study, prisons. Goffman's ideas shed insight on the setting and context of prisons whereby he paints a picture of the restrictions and confinements characterizing these establishments. As noted by Weinstein (1982), Goffman's work is one of the primary sociological studies examining the situation and experiences of inmates—individuals residing inside total institutions. By sketching the characteristics and features of total institutions, Goffman (1961) offers a way of understanding what these institutions make of the inmates, as well as what the inmates make of life inside these establishments. Importantly, we apply Goffman's theoretical conceptualizations not to theorize or analyze the purpose of prison, but rather to frame the experiences of the men.

Goffman's (1961) conceptualizations related to total institutions are of value when examining initiatives within prison, as insights can be drawn to help understand what role and impact prison theatre has on criminalized individuals. The dynamic relationship between criminalized individuals, prison, and theatre can be intricately understood

---

2 Within symbolic interactionism, identities are seen as being formed and shaped through social interactions.

through the conceptual developments offered by Goffman (1961). First, his ideas on total institutions help to cognize and illustrate life, or experiences, of being confined inside total institutions. Furthermore, Goffman's concepts related to total institutions shed light into some of the resisting strategies employed by inmates to cope with the constraints of these institutions. Goffman's work speaks to the importance of engaging with questions of space and confinement and allows for us to reflect on the context in which prison theatre operates to gain a better understanding of the experiences of the men with WHoS.

There has undoubtedly been shifting discourses around incarceration, particularly in criminology where the concept of the total institution may not perfectly capture the image of the modern prison. That is, the application of Goffman's conceptualization of total institutions may be regarded as dated given that it is not reflective of the modern prison system where restrictions are less total, and the separation between the inside and outside are less dichotomous or distinct (Ellis 2021; Farrington 1992; Martin and Mitchelson 2009). Notably, a more contemporary way in which Goffman's theoretical work has evolved amongst criminological scholarship is through the lens of porosity rather than totality. Building on the work of Crewe (2009), Ellis (2021) adjusts the notion of prisons as total institutions through the recognition of modern prisons having openings or entry points whereby contact may flow and permeate from the outside in, and the inside out. Notwithstanding this contemporary perspective, Ellis (2021) and other emerging research do not seek to dismantle the paradigm of total institutions or imply that prisons are open. Rather, it is to reframe our understanding of how modern prisons operate, which may not be designed as total institutions in the same way as in the past.

Despite the emergence of more contemporary interpretations of prisons, scholars continue to contextualize their research in terms of prison as a total institution. Of significance is the recognition that elements of total institutions do still stand and remain evident in current day institutions. Marked by encompassing tendencies where individuals are separated from the larger society and lead an enclosed, formally administered way of life, we recognize that modern day prisons retain the fundamental features characterizing total institutions (Goffman 1961). Parallel to Goffman's illustration of the total institution, the modern prison remains to be conceptualized by criminologists as fundamentally confining (Hancock and Jewkes 2011; Carlen 2005; Crewe and Ievins 2020; Crewe 2011). Additionally, we view Goffman's theorization as holding the recognition of "porosity" through his conceptualization of secondary adjustments and presence of specialists, as will be applied in later chapters. As such, Goffman's (1961) conceptualizations related to total institutions remain pertinent to understanding the role and impact prison theatre has on criminalized individuals.

Alongside Goffman's (1961) conceptualizations, to appreciate and understand the nuances of the men's experiences, we consider the social aspect of prison by drawing conceptual developments around the social structures of prison as they relate to the inmate culture (Clemmer 1940). Theoretical underpinnings around prison inmate culture, ethos, or as Crewe (2009) describes the "social world" of prison, is a valuable perspective to adopt as the experiences of participants in prison theatre are likely to be conceptualized and defined against the normative social context of prison. For example, in Chapter 3 we draw on theorizations around prison masculinity to capture the emotional environment characterizing prison and how theatre-making disrupts the rigidity of it (Ricciardelli 2014a; 2014b). In Chapter 4, we draw on theorizations on the inmate culture to illustrate the unique sense of community and connectedness that WHoS affords the men.

While the institution fundamentally mandates the life of prisoners—as Goffman (1961) would assert—it is essential to recognize that prison life is also largely shaped by the social and normative behaviours set out by the prisoners themselves. The theoretical consideration of the inmate culture began with Donald Clemmer's investigation of the inmate community in his pioneering work, *The Prison Community*. Clemmer (1940, 270) introduces the term *prisonization* to describe, "[…] the taking on in greater or less degree of the folkways, mores, customs, and general culture of the penitentiary." In prison, narratives and expectations are set out about how one should behave, known as the prison inmate culture. Despite the covert and unofficial status of the inmate culture, it is an aspect of prison life that is widely understood, enforced, and reproduced by inmates (Haney 2011).

Within the penological literature, notions of masculinity are conceptualized as inherently entrenched and embedded within the inmate culture and social system (Britton 2003; Crewe 2014; De Viggiani 2012; Evans and Wallace 2008; Jewkes 2005; Newton 1994; Phillips 2001; Ricciardelli 2015; Sykes 1958). More specifically, the behaviours, attitudes, and values associated with the inmate culture are moulded around dominant displays of masculinity as well as an exaggerated version of it. R. W. Connell's (1995) seminal development of hegemonic masculinity stands as the most enduring and widely recognized theorization for understanding the inmate prison culture. Applied to the study of masculinity, hegemonic masculinity is understood to be the socially idealized expression of manhood (Connell 1987; Messerschmidt 1993; Connell and Messerschmidt 2005). Scholars such as Sabo et al. (2001) have theorized that the unisex environment of prison amplifies hierarchical relations that both fuel and reproduce hegemonic ideals (as cited in Ricciardelli 2015). In prison where masculinity is continuously contested and the opportunity for prisoners to assert their masculine status is limited, the expression becomes redefined into an intensified version of the hegemonic ideal (Bandyopadhyay 2006; Haney 2011; Karp 2010; Phillips 2001; Ricciardelli 2014b; Rymhs 2012; Toch 1998). The inmate culture has been observed and conceptualized to enforce an intensified or exaggerated version of masculinity, known as hyper-masculinity (Jewkes 2005; Karp 2010; Toch 1998).

The inmate culture and the social context of prison can undoubtedly be seen as linked by the "umbilical cord of masculinity" portrayed in the larger society (Sim 1994, 115). While the assertion of the masculine ideal in the inmate culture may be seen as a reflection of wider societal notions of hegemonic masculinity (Irwin and Cressey 1962), the prison social context itself is also a distinctly gendered environment that fosters an intensified, hyper-masculine ideal (Ugelvik 2014; Sykes 1958). That is, we recognize that the overall social environment within prisons is contoured by both societal norms and the prison context itself. For this reason, we integrate theories and conceptualizations of prison and general culture within them so that a more comprehensive understanding of the impacts of WHoS on the lives of criminalized individuals can be established. This pushes us to understand how the men navigate doing theatre within the confines and norms of prison.

CHAPTER 3

Freedom from Within

> *WHoS was a lot of fun, it took up a lot of time, so it made those four months go fast, and that's a good thing. It's a big commitment, and then when it's over you get a bit depressed, and you miss it. But I look forward to it every year [...] Words just can't describe, like those two hours in the evenings on some days, you just can't wait for them to come.*
>
> – Seth, formerly incarcerated WHoS participant

3.1. Escaping the Venue

Laughter, music, cheering, and overall excitement—these are some of the feelings and sounds that fill the room when the WHoS men are preparing for a production. A notable theme emerging from the narratives of the men relates to the feelings they experience from being involved with the theatre company. Expressed against the monotonous environment and life in prison, many describe their involvement with WHoS as being a form of detachment from the prison context. Throughout the experiences shared by the men, they speak of how being a part of WHoS is an elevated, joyous time. In particular, putting together a production and performing it in front of a live audience is a fundamental aspect of the theatre company that many of the men attribute with heightened emotions and energy. As Michael, an incarcerated WHoS participant, expresses, "the excitement you feel in show nights, we get excited, we're happy that people are coming and the shows are sold out, so that's a good thing. There is a lot of excitement!"

Despite the feelings of anxiety and fear many of the men identify when it comes to having to perform on stage in front of a public audience, the men routinely describe their significant sense of excitement as a euphoric experience. As Logan, an incarcerated WHoS participant, explains, "I just feel good because I see the audience's reaction. It's really like a euphoria, like your body is charged up." For Joe, another incarcerated WHoS participant, the positive feelings he has from taking part in WHoS is principally meaningful. As he describes, "Once I did the first show, that was it. I was in love with that because it showed me that I didn't need booze or drugs to have fun." The sense of joy and excitement associated with WHoS and with performing theatre is echoed in many of the men's testimonies. For Samuel, witnessing the positive feelings and energy of the WHoS cast after having assisted backstage during his first year is what sparked his interest in getting more involved in the theatre company: "You can feel their enthusiasm as they came off the stage and that positive energy and I was kind of like, 'hmm, that's nice!'—because I can hear the applause from the audience and all the positive feedback from the people that just watched the show" (Samuel, incarcerated WHoS participant).

Beyond the performance aspect, the process of theatre-making and the elements of WHoS that lead to the final production are also experiences that the men associate with elevated positive feelings. The men speak of the enjoyment and fun they experience during the WHoS workshops and during the processes leading up to the production, such as the rehearsals and the design aspects. For example, when reflecting on the WHoS workshops, Karl expresses how these workshops represented times when the men can experience a sense of relief while engaging in entertaining activities. As he explains, "the workshops are fun, and it's a time to let go of our physique, to kind of put something special on our faces and just goofing around, making funny noises" (Karl, incarcerated WHoS participant). Seth reinforces this when he talks about his first experience in the workshops. As he describes, "when I came out, I was giggling, and laughing—I had a good time, and that's when I really started to enjoy what was going on" (Seth, formerly incarcerated WHoS participant).

The experiences of the men at WHoS parallel the findings of previous studies that have also identified the engaging feature of prison theatre (Brewster 2010; Merrill and Frigon 2015; Shailor 2011; Tocci 2007). From an imaginative criminological approach, WHoS offers a space of transgression for the men, as the restrictions and deprivations associated with imprisonment and the openness and flexibility of doing theatre offer a notable juxtaposition. The creative space and imaginative freedom associated with theatre-making is largely noted within the theatre literature (Branders 2023; Shailor 2011). However, extending beyond the identification of the uplifting experiences, the theme emerging from the men's experiences with WHoS uncovers how such accounts may be understood as offering a sense of release and detachment from the prison context. In line with Lucas (2020), the sense of freedom or escapism experienced by the men should not be interpreted as liberation. Rather, it is that the men's involvement with WHoS and the process of creating affords them a sense of transcendence, expanded imaginative capacity, and the potential to focus themselves away from the prison environment.

Prison, as conceptualized through Goffman (1961), involves routinized activities, scheduled tasks, and an overall regimented environment. WHoS, as demonstrated by the men, appears to offer an environment that is intrinsically different to this. The men contrast the positive and exhilarating environment of WHoS against the mundaneness of prison. As Kevin expresses, "Prison is a very toxic and negative environment. You make what you want to make out of this environment [...] but WHoS it is a very happy place [...] by the time the last shows come together and everyone sits in the circle and shares their experience; it's totally joyous" (Kevin, incarcerated WHoS participant).

Goffman's (1961) theorization of removal activities may be applied to understand this break in the prison context. Goffman advances his ideas on life within total institutions by recognizing how inmates partake in certain practices to acquire elements of freedom and uphold the restrictive environment, known as secondary adjustments. These adjustments exemplify ways of coping with the environment and represent ways in which the individual stands apart from the institution (Goffman 1961). Removal activities are seen as particular types of secondary adjustments that allow the inmates to disconnect from the regimented institutional environment. Goffman (1961) conceptualizes removal activities because of their ability to create a sense of separation and release from the institutional atmosphere. The significance of removal activities comes from the function they serve for the inmates. As Goffman describes, they are: "[...] Sufficiently engrossing and exciting to lift the participant out of himself, making him oblivious for the time being to his actual situation. If the ordinary activities in total institutions can be said to torture time, those activities mercifully kill it." (Goffman 1961, 68).

WHoS affords the men an opportunity to remove themselves from the normalizations of prison and retreat into a context that is regarded as positive and uplifting. As Armin, a formerly incarcerated WHoS participant describes, these experiences in WHoS, "get the prison out of you." Similarly to how Goffman (1961) conceptualizes removal activities as practice or engagement that create a sense of release from the institutional atmosphere, WHoS too may be understood as a form of escapism from prison. Many of the men describe how WHoS has assisted them in coping with the institutional atmosphere, or as Zane, an incarcerated WHoS participant, describes it, in helping them "decompress" from prison. Andrew, a formerly incarcerated WHoS participant, elaborates on this understanding of WHoS:

> Without WHoS, I don't know what I would have done. It's stressful psychologically, emotionally being there [in prison], and how do you deal with that pressure or those thoughts, whatever it is. So, some people it's drugs, exercise, hit the gym, running, wood working, pen pals, whatever. So, you have some kind of focus, some kind of hobby—that release valve—and so what better than theatre! (Andrew, formerly incarcerated WHoS participant)

Andrew's account illustrates the constrictions and challenges faced by imprisonment. However, participating in WHoS offers the men a way to mitigate these pressures by removing themselves, though temporarily, from the taxing environment of prison. At WHoS, participants experience a form of freedom whereby they are able to experience positive emotions and feelings, as described earlier, which are uncommon in prison. As Dylan, a formerly incarcerated WHoS participant, highlights, "when the show is over there is all this excitement in the room, like that emotion—you don't get that in prison." The removal or escape the men attribute to WHoS is similar to Shailor's (2011) identification of theatre practices being places of sanctuary from their normal prison surroundings.

WHoS can be further understood as a form of removal activity. A commonly expressed experience is how the men do not feel like they are in prison when taking part in WHoS. Jake speaks to this when he reflects on his involvement with WHoS: "When you are involved in it, you are working on something that has nothing to do with the prison, nothing at all to do with the prison. […] and it was that form of escape. And of course, the outside people that came in, again, they're not the prison people—they're different people" (Jake, formerly incarcerated WHoS participant). Jake's words speak to the contrasting environment between WHoS and the prison context, whereby the men are afforded the chance to take part in an initiative that is not mandated by the prison and involves interaction with outsiders. Together, these aspects of WHoS further consolidate how WHoS can be understood as a form of escape from the prison context. Dylan reinforces this when he speaks of WHoS: "When you are there you kind of get transported out of the whole prison and the politics. There is a guard presence, but they are not involved with it—so it's like okay this is your one little break from the monotony of prison life. So, when you are there it's kind of like you are not there" (Dylan, formerly incarcerated WHoS participant).

In Goffman's (1961, 68) conceptualization of removal activities he notes, "[…] if the ordinary activities in total institution can be said to torture time, those activities mercifully kill it." This resonates with many of the men's accounts as many of them express how WHoS gave them something with which to occupy their time, to keep them busy, and notably, something to look forward to. Indeed, all the men express how WHoS is a big commitment that takes up many hours of their day over the course of several months. For many of the men, participating in WHoS helps pass the time in a productive way. As Jake, a formerly incarcerated WHoS participant, puts it, "it got to be a time pit because it was a place to escape. When you were there, you weren't in jail." Overall, evident from the experiences and narratives of the men, WHoS offers a form of escapism or removal from the monotony of prison and allows the men a sense of relief from the context and routinization of prison.

Figure 3.1. Bollywood dance in *Time Waits for No One* (2014 production). *Source:* Jam Hamidi for William Head on Stage.

3.2. Breaking the Scene

> For me, being able to express myself, the happy times and the bad times—I think guys need to be able to convey what they're feeling, and not be ashamed of it and not be made fun of or anything. And that all plays into the growth I've experienced through WHoS.
>
> –Kevin, incarcerated WHoS participant

From the concrete walls and cold rooms, one thing that almost all prisons have in common is the dryness in the atmosphere and, like the physical environment, the carceral space is also characterized by emotional dryness or apathy. The discussions with the men continuously point to the difference between WHoS and overarching normative standards in prison that calls for the inhibition of emotional expression. As will be explored, the men's narratives around the emotional growth experienced through WHoS is highlighted in several ways.

Previous research on prison theatre has recognized the capacity for theatre in aiding individuals with engaging with their emotions (Landy 1994; Nicholson 2014; Pensalfini 2019). However, the experiences of the men of WHoS shed particular insight on how this emotional engagement and expression becomes of imminent importance in the context of prison. Within the penological literature, it is conceptualized that notions of masculinity are inherently entrenched and embedded within the inmate culture and social system of prison (Britton 2003; Crewe 2014; De Viggiani 2012; Evans and Wallace 2008; Jewkes 2005; Newton 1994; Phillips 2001; Ricciardelli 2015; Sykes 1958). More specifically, the behaviours, attitudes, and values associated with the inmate culture are moulded around dominant displays of masculinity as well as an exaggerated version of it.

As theorized by Toch (1998), prison is a hyper-masculine environment where an inflated or hyper version of manhood is both promoted and reinforced. As illustrated through the narratives of the WHoS men, the dominant prison culture does not support overt displays of emotional expression. In describing the emotional atmosphere of prison, Kevin asserts how, "Sitting in prison you don't show emotion. Like when you're having a conversation with somebody you don't have a smile on your face, even when you're taking pictures you don't smile—you don't, everything is suppressed" (Kevin, incarcerated WHoS participant).

In this regard, displays of domination and aggression are reinforced and perpetrated while exhibitions of vulnerability and emotional expression are discouraged. Many of the men spoke of "guards," "barriers," "walls," and "layers" that they built for themselves in prison to inhibit or otherwise conceal their emotions. These accounts are reflective of the theorizations of fronting and masking, which have been identified as defining features associated with the hegemonic, hyper-masculine nature of the inmate culture (Crewe et al. 2014). That is, as much as the hyper-masculinity of the inmate culture entails the adoption of rampant displays of dominance, physicality, and toughness, it also compels the inhibition of other behaviours that are regarded as subordinate. The inmate culture rejects displays of softness, gentleness, fear, kindness, or love (Carceral 2003; Karp 2010; Sabo et al. 2001; Seymour 2003; Toch 1992). Such emotional expressions not only undermine the masculine ideal, but they may be regarded as indicators of vulnerability and weakness (De Viggiani 2012; Haney 2011; Karp 2010; Seymour 2003). Adopting a tough, hyper-masculine façade characterized by emotional concealment and suppression shows conformity and is widely understood through the conceptualizations of "wearing masks" and "putting up fronts" (Crewe et al. 2013; De Viggiani 2012; Jewkes 2005; Karp 2010).

The concepts of masking and fronting have been widely recognized and used in the literature as a frame to the masculinity characterizing the prison inmate culture. This book specifically adopts the conceptual frameworks developed by Crewe et al. (2014) in their study examining the emotional geography of prison life. Masking and fronting represent two distinct but complementary strategies of subscribing to prison masculinity. Fronting is understood as the overt display of certain emotions or characteristics to communicate one's masculine potential. On the other hand, masking in this context is understood as the suppression or hiding of emotions that may be regarded as indicative of vulnerability, weakness, or fear. As Crewe et al. (2014, 64) affirm, when it comes to fronting and masking in relation to emotional expression in prisons, "this is the difference between cultivating or presenting a version of the (emotional) self that is inauthentic, and concealing or holding in a version that is authentic." That is, fronting involves the generating and displaying of emotions whereas masking, as its name suggests, involves the concealment of emotions and anything that may appear as feminine or otherwise not in line with the hyper-masculine ideal. Taken together, the social environment of prison can be understood as a unique social context characterized by a culture that is largely woven by hegemonic, hyper-masculine strands.

Both fronting and masking may be applied to understand the accounts of the men participating in WHoS, given that many of the men describe how in prison they often inflate displays of masculinity—such as toughness—while at the same time conceal traces of vulnerabilities. Karl, an incarcerated WHoS participant, exemplifies the presence of this masculine façade when he describes how, "normally we try not to show emotion, we try not to act tough and stuff, but we go to this place [WHoS] to kind of just have fun and be ourselves."

Despite the pressure to maintain a masculine façade given the social normative system that is reinforced in prison, the participants highlight the dormancy that this façade has when they are in WHoS. Kevin speaks to this when he describes how the men shed their layers and drop their guard when they are in WHoS:

> Guys get emotional in there, they talk about their lives, they relate their lives to the scenes, and you got to be supportive [...] The guys shed their layers after a little bit of time in there and that's a huge shift in a lot of guys who have done long time because you got guys that come from very different walks of life and you

got to drop the guard [...] I think once guys start shedding those layers and start being able to feel and talk about their stuff, I think that's a big shift in a person's ability to manage themselves. (Kevin, incarcerated WHoS participant)

Reflective of Kevin's words and the narratives of the participants, WHoS provides an opportunity for the men to drop the fronts and masks that they so often maintain throughout prison. WHoS allows the men to connect with each other on a personal and emotional level. The camaraderie that develops between the men at WHoS, as is explored in Chapter 4, fosters a climate where dominant prison inmate culture assumes less relevance and the men are able to reveal aspects of their authentic self without masks or fronts, with some degree of security. As demonstrated, several men spoke of the relevance of this in aiding them with their ability to understand and empathize with both the experiences and emotions of others.

WHoS can be understood as offering a unique emotional domain to the dominant prison culture. This is parallel to recent research in criminology looking at the emotional geography of prisons and the presence of what Crewe et al. (2014) identify as distinct or differentiated emotion zones. Certain areas within the prison are recognized to carry softer emotional atmospheres whereby the hyper-masculine nature of the dominant prison culture is partially suspended (Crewe et al. 2014). The literature has identified some of these zones to include the privacy of prisoners' cells (Jewkes 2005) and family visiting areas (Crewe et al. 2013; Moran 2013). Likewise, the participants' narratives in this study demonstrate how WHoS may also be understood as a differentiated emotional domain to the dominant prison system. Drawing from the experiences of the men, the emotional disclosure that WHoS permits appears to offer a sense of relief for many of the men. Having to constantly uphold a masculine front and mask their emotions appears to be a challenge that many of the men face.

Many spoke of the desire to move past this hyper-masculine bravado they put on and point to the significance of WHoS in helping them do so. In considering the emotional robustness required for prison, Kevin explains how:

It's not a good place to be for me, guarded all the time. I want to be able to be like me, and I don't want to be the guy that's going to be cold and not receptive to a person when they're talking. So with this whole theatre stuff you have to shed those layers and you get comfortable with being able to convey and deal with your own emotions […] Like, I always thought that whatever I did or experienced, nobody else experienced, but it's until I started sharing it with people, everyone experiences the same thing. (Kevin, incarcerated WHoS participant)

Jake reinforces this when he talks about how WHoS has helped him with his emotional expression:

WHoS has helped me on my journey to get from where I was when I walked in, to where I am now. Which is being able to express feelings, which I suppressed for years and years and years. You know, it has so many benefits to it. The biggest one is your emotional growth that you get out of it. Being able to trust yourself to be strong enough to share your feelings, and realize that everybody has feelings, and not everyone is going to jump on and crush them—and they will share their feelings with your feelings and it's a way of connecting and bonding. I think that's one of the biggest ones. (Jake, formerly incarcerated WHoS participant)

While the participants' testimonies demonstrate the emotional growth they experience through WHoS by being able to emotionally disclose and show vulnerability, it is important to recognize that this does not come with ease. The men share how they felt initial discomfort with having to open up or show feelings given that they are accustomed to emotional inhibition. For example, Logan describes how showing emotion is difficult for him, but that being in-character when he is acting allowed him to display emotion with more ease:

Well, it's weird because like when you're wearing costume it's easier to do it, then when you're standing there by yourself […] I felt more exposed. But, when I had the mask on and the other things I have to wear, that stuff is kind of like a shield where I can just become this character out here and that no one can really see that it's me. So, that's like my false sense of insecurity. (Logan, incarcerated WHoS participant)

WHoS places the men in a setting in which they are able to engage with their emotions. In acting and performing different character roles in the production, the men must embody the feelings and emotions of their character, and in turn project it to the audience. As highlighted by the men, achieving this often involves the voyage of drawing on connections between the character and themselves. Jackson, an incarcerated WHoS participant, explains how he is able to embody the feelings of desolation associated with his character by relating it to his life, "I projected a lot of things I went through as a child because I can relate to the character in the sense that I had a bad relationship with my father [...] I know how it feels, so I was able to express that." Logan echoes Jackson's experience when he shares how he sees his character's experience of abandonment resembling his own life story. As he describes, "when I'm acting out this role there is something inside of me being expressed through that character and the next day when I wake up, I feel lighter" (Logan, incarcerated WHoS participant).

Evidenced from accounts of the participants, the emotional engagement that WHoS stimulates becomes particularly pronounced when productions are written or devised by the men. In many WHoS productions, such as *Sleeping Giants* in 2016 and *Time Waits for No One* in 2014, the productions integrate personal experiences or sentimental stories from the men themselves. Amongst many, some of the personal narratives that are incorporated into WHoS productions include childhood memories, stories of separation, and experiences with heartbreak or parental abandonment, in addition to the incorporation of elements from Indigenous culture. These stories or elements that the men can express through WHoS productions carry sentimental value or emotional significance to them. Several men express how the production—including the preceding workshops and reflective exercises used to draw on their experiences—are emotionally healing. Through WHoS, the men are able to reflect on their stories and in turn, work through their emotions—which many of them express to have been customarily sheltered in prison. Accordingly, WHoS can be understood as offering a form of emotional release for those involved that, from an imaginative criminological perspective, transgresses the prison context (Branders 2023). While the literature has evidently highlighted the masculine aura within prisons, the men's accounts shed light on how masculinity can come to be renegotiated and deconstructed within WHoS. Brandon's experience as an actor in WHoS helps illustrate this:

> So, my role was coming out from a point of loss, the dissociation from my family, from my loved ones, which is very real for me [...]

> It was me expressing what I feel about experiences that I've had. I had a lot of loss to reflect on, to lean on. I cried every single show, which gave me an opportunity to show my vulnerability, and not really be concerned with the judgment that comes with it. It's a difficult thing to come out and stand in front of this crowd and just leak when it's really not what we're meant to do here. You know, we bark at people, we do whatever, but to sit there and leak in front of people—it's difficult—but that's what I did […] We are not used to men standing up on stage and crying, it's just not the norm. (Brandon, incarcerated WHoS participant)

Brandon's account is significant not only because it reveals the emotional catharsis associated with relating to the characters and stories in the production, but also beyond that, it is demonstrative of a reoccurring narrative that is woven in almost all the accounts of the men, which is the emotional expression WHoS permits and the unique emotional geography it offers.

CHAPTER 4

The Ensemble

> *In WHoS and when we get out there [on stage], we're a team—it's not me by myself, it's a team that goes on stage. And if you forget your lines or drop your lines, the other actors are there to support you [...] So ya, as a team we always seem to succeed and that's one of the things I really like about being a part of the WHoS production, it's a team effort and everyone puts in their part, and we work as one unit, and we don't want to see anybody fail. A lot of times we put our differences aside because we are not from the same backgrounds, or religion, or even institutions, and politics inside the institution—like whether you're in on this type of charge—your index offence. We put all these differences aside, and we get together and we produce a show for the public. So, I think that's one of the most appealing things about WHoS—for me anyways.*
>
> – Samuel, incarcerated WHoS participant

4.1. Connecting Inside

The beauty of WHoS is not limited to the performances themselves as it is evident in the very process of theatre-making. For the weeks passed at William Head Institution, Thana had the opportunity to spend much of her time backstage with the men of WHoS as they eagerly prepared for their performances. Hours before audience seats start filling up and the performance begins, the men are backstage getting ready. What we noticed was that no one was on their own; all the men were working together like bees in a beehive. Helping each other get into their costumes, putting make-up on each other's faces and bodies, rehearsing lines, making each other coffee—regardless of what it was, the men were in it together. The continuous cordial occurrences witnessed backstage at WHoS became illustrative of the collaborative environment and comradeship that are woven in the men's accounts.

The capacity of WHoS to unite and bring the men together is one of the most prominent themes evident from the interviews with the men of WHoS. The narratives of the men routinely point to the collaborative environment where everyone needs to work together for the company to operate and for a production to come to life. Andrew uses the analogy of a meal to illustrate how being a part of WHoS entails a joint effort from all those involved:

> I use the example of the meal. The theatre or performance is the meal. And so there are people who wash the dishes, there are people who cook the food, there are people that serve the meal, and there are people that sweep up afterwards. Every job is important! So, if the floor is dirty or the lights don't turn on, or if the lines are not read, chairs aren't set up properly—if somebody screws up we all screw up, you know it all falls apart and it all cascades down. And so everybody is helping everybody and that's the community of WHoS—not just on stage. (Andrew, formerly incarcerated WHoS participant)

The men of WHoS are brought together by the common goal of putting on a production. That is, it is not a one-man show, but rather they are all working together to stage the play and doing what it takes to keep the show running. Importantly, this connectedness and collaboration that is present in WHoS does not begin backstage, but rather months before the production is open to the public. During these months, the men spend time writing, rehearsing, designing costumes, and working to make the production happen. As Joe describes, "The entire process of WHoS brings people together—not just the performance: That's what WHoS does—like this play didn't start a month ago, this play started right after last Christmas. They started to have meetings, ideas and playing silly games […] but by doing all that, that's what brings people together" (Joe, incarcerated WHoS participant). The connectedness characterizing the men's experiences with WHoS resonates with the understandings developed from case studies on prisoners participating in arts-based intervention programs in Scottish prisons, whereby Tett et al. (2012) note the interconnections and relationships that theatre practices help foster amongst individuals.

The accounts of the WHoS men shed light on the connections and bonds that are formed from being a part of a theatre company. The men underscore the significance of being able to connect with others on an initiative that is prosocial and positive. Several of the men make note of how most of their teamwork and relationships formed in prison are often negatively centred. For example, Lincoln, a formerly incarcerated WHoS participant, reflects on how his best relationships were often with drugs and negative "criminal minded" individuals but, through WHoS, he was given people who were set on one main goal that everyone can agree on, which he describes as, "[…] a good show and good times."

Beyond this, activities offered within institutions are often individualized or otherwise focused on the individual themselves, rather than a group. Unlike most activities, which are often characterized by limited significant interactions with others, WHoS allows individuals to come together for a collective undertaking and step away from the individualistic rhetoric of prison. As Thomas highlights:

> There are a lot of people that stay in their rooms and do nothing— and they've been doing it since probably max and medium [security institutions]—because they are so insular. There is not a lot of interaction other than probably sports, card playing, and things like that. And so WHoS is a totally different thing, it's a different beast in itself; everyone gets together and produces something that's creative. (Thomas, incarcerated WHoS participant)

While the alliance associated with creating theatre and being a part of WHoS is, as Jake describes, "[…] closer camaraderie than you ever would find in any other prison setting," the men working together is not an easy or harmonious process. The men continually voiced and shared the difficulties and challenges of having to negotiate and work with others as a cohesive group. As Jayden, an incarcerated WHoS participant, explains, "there are some people [who] are very rough around the edges and it's sometimes really hard to be around them, but you're just like, I got to let it go for things to work." In having to work as a group, the participants share a host of challenges that arise in WHoS that the men try to work through, such as individuals falling short of their tasks, or individuals not being responsive to feedback. However, the men routinely express how the collectivist nature of WHoS that necessitates them to work through and overcome these interpersonal obstacles has proven to be an invaluable experience for them. Sammy speaks to this when he conveys the patience he has learned to develop from having to work with others:

> For myself, establishing more of that patience and communicating with people and not getting aggressive—I think that was a lesson for me. It is—especially in a prison setting, you know what I mean, it can get pretty fucking stupid over nothing, people start acting very immature. You can tell when a lot of guys are having difficulty working with people. (Sammy, incarcerated WHoS participant)

Seth, a formerly incarcerated WHoS participant, further highlights this when he explains how the cooperation and teamwork he developed from his experience with WHoS resonates with him to this day, "WHoS made me understand that life is a team game, you got to work together. And now, even when I'm working, I ask the other guys what do you think of this? I never did that before!" Beyond bringing individuals together where they can collectively be a part of a team, the collaborative nature of WHoS frames an environment where the men are able to challenge and put aside many of their judgments and intolerance towards each other. In working on a unified goal and purpose, the men express how they are compelled to come together and not let their differences overshadow the theatre-making process of WHoS. Brandon expresses how WHoS helped him look past his negative views towards those around him:

> As much as I want you to not view me as a monster, I will take my own judgments and look at the person beside me and judge him. And WHoS has really kind of forced my hand to look at that […] either I can hold on to my own judgments and not really be a team player, or I could put that aside and be productive and be something positive in WHoS. I don't want to hinder the WHoS process at all, and that means I had to put down some

of the judgments that I carry. (Brandon, incarcerated WHoS participant)

In discussing the presence of intolerances towards each other, as well as the challenges they must in turn negotiate through, the men's narratives continually reveal how many of these preconceived judgments towards each other stem from the social normative context of prison. Through these discussions, it is helpful to draw on the theoretical underpinnings on the "social world" of prison for the development of nuanced understandings (Crewe 2009). Understandings around the prison inmate culture and ethos offer a valuable perspective to understanding the experiences of men at WHoS given that they are conceptualized and defined against the normative social context of prison.

Throughout the interviews, the men at WHoS allude to the presence of what they identify as "prison culture," "prison politics," or the "con code." While multifaceted, the men often explicate tensions and difficulties in having to associate with the "different classes of inmates," which they explain as relating to different offences. This resembles the pecking order of the inmate culture in prisons that have been identified in previous studies on carceral spaces done by Karp (2010), Jewkes (2005), and Sabo et al. (2001). While the normative culture of prisoners tends to reinforce and perpetuate an environment where interpersonal relations are often based on differences, hierarchies, and criminal past, WHoS offers an opportunity for them to begin to break the intolerances and prejudices they hold towards each other, which are moulded by the con code or inmate culture. As Brandon explains:

> Being able to work or having to work with some of the men that I was working with, you know really challenged me on my willingness to hang on to a lot of the con code that I carry. Like I'm not able to put it all down today, I've been in for almost 25 years—but I don't want to believe in the con code anymore! [...] So it really forced me to look at that, and the value of hanging on to those values. Sometimes when you've done something in a certain way for an extended period of time, it's just hard to put it down—even when you've grown beyond it, it's just hard to put down—you know the first thing that comes to your mouth is some sort of lash, some sort of criticism. So, it was difficult not to be that way,

especially when one is a child molester, one raped—it's difficult, so it really forced me to challenge how far I wanted to carry that. So, this is a huge step forward for me, to just really not judge them anymore. (Brandon, incarcerated WHoS participant)

Brandon's involvement reveals a shared experience expressed amongst the men, which is the difficulty of having to put aside their judgments and views. The normalization of the participants to the con code or culture in prison is illustrative of Clemmer's (1940) theoretical understanding of prisonization. Through their incarceration, the men have come to adopt and accept the views that are enforced and perpetuated by the prison culture. For many of the men, the extended experience of being incarcerated makes looking past this social normative system particularly relevant. As Samuel explains:

I think that over years of being in maximum and medium security prisons and the integral violence that happens inside there in the prisons—I think after years of that and then coming down to minimum, I did need to make some serious adjustments. You know you have this bravado of don't look at me, don't talk to me, you're less than me […] So for me, in here, getting involved in the play and interacting with guys that I don't really normally interact with gave me a chance to open up and not be so guarded from others, and change my belief system. So those adjustments are slow and they are work in progress, but I still value them and I still work on them daily, and I think it will be beneficial when I get back in the community. (Samuel, incarcerated WHoS participant)

In WHoS the men are challenged or compelled to not let their preconceived judgments of each other overshadow the theatre process where individuals are part of a team and a goal that extends beyond their individual self. WHoS allows the men to re-imagine themselves as a collective, as a group. Jackson reinforces this narrative when he speaks of his experience:

I've been in since I was 16 years old and I've preconditioned myself to live in prison and abide by the con code. So immersing myself in this situation it really put myself out there to surround myself with the sex offenders and other sorts of people. But, once I got passed that, I haven't looked back. It was hard though. But after I put all that stuff to the side I just focused on the team [...] I mean, I even gained respect for some of these men—and I need that, because I can't be looking at people because they're this or they're that if I want to be a productive member of society. I'm starting to look at people for just people right now—as opposed to this guy is sex offender, and this guy is this, this guy is that—I'm just like whatever, this guy is my co-actor. (Jackson, incarcerated WHoS participant)

In coming together through WHoS, the men are exposed to different aspects of each other that challenge their own prejudices and help them negotiate new understandings. WHoS offers a lesion or intermission to the prison culture whereby interpersonal relationships can be constructed on communion rather than on the emphasis of differences. Dylan, a formerly incarcerated WHoS participant, illustrates this when he reflects on the social atmosphere of WHoS, "I was very judgmental [...] but, as the play gets developing, we let those things go and it's all left outside of there because that space was where everyone was just human—and we were friendly to each other." The level of connection formed at WHoS allows the men to begin to detach themselves from social normative understandings of prison while at the same time allowing them to recognize the insignificance of their perceived differences. Joe's words elucidate this:

In prison there are different cultures; there are offences, there's religion, there's gangs—all kinds of different aspects of prison. And what I found is that when people are in the WHoS, that kind of takes a backseat—not always, but most of the time it takes a backseat and it gives people a chance to get to see that we are not all that different, really. And some guys realize that and it makes a difference in their life because that's when they start changing and that's when they start going like, "Ok well maybe there's more to this person, there's better here." And if that happens for one guy, it's big. (Joe, incarcerated WHoS participant)

The community artists that are involved with WHoS help foster a collective space for the men. In the final hour before the men got on stage, the artists encourage everyone to form a circle and hold hands. As we stood with the men in the circle during our visit to WHoS, we could not help but notice how these men, of all backgrounds, histories, and walks of life, are coming together during these moments, connecting with one another. Feelings of sincere regard and warmth filled the space in the circle the men formed, as each person, one by one, shared appreciation statements and words of encouragement. Reflecting on this ritual from one year's production, Dave, an incarcerated WHoS participant, describes how, "during those moments there was a real sense of community and transcending of prison politics, and criminal past—all this". While some men describe the communal atmosphere as being transitory or limited to the context of WHoS, many typically spoke of the extension of these bonds. Individuals who take on similar acting roles, work on parts of the set together, or are involved in the same WHoS productions over the years often express the cultivation of rapport and friendships amongst each other. Given their mutual involvement with WHoS, former participants often spoke of the continuation of the friendships they developed through WHoS being carried over to the outside.

Taken together, the communion characterizing WHoS helps promote new understandings for the men whereby the prejudices and judgments inherent in the prison culture can come to be contested. While the collaborative capacity of theatre practices is well recognized in the literature (Moller 2003; Thompson 2003), the men's experiences shed unique insight on how WHoS helps challenge the views and judgments often held by those incarcerated. Through the process of co-creation, the men of WHoS establish community and solidarity. Expanding beyond prison theatre, this finding bears relevance for the broader criminological literature. Despite the widespread recognition of prisons having a social world, there is limited understanding on how this social normative system can be attenuated. Prison theatre, such as WHoS, may offer a means through which the prison culture can be partially suspended. This is particularly relevant given that many of the men necessitate their desire to move past the social normative system perpetrated within prison. Prison politics and the overall con code are so interlaced in the prison context that the men often express their disbelief in how WHoS can bring them together. As Zane, an incarcerated WHoS participant, shares, "I am so blown away that everybody can put their guns down and say, you know what, we're in this together, we're going to go on stage and we're going to do this!"

Figure 4.1. The men working together to create visual effects in *Antigone* (2017 production).
Source: Jam Hamidi for William Head on Stage.

4.2. Community Connection

> The volunteers they come in and its endless support! It brings such warmth to each and everybody, they bring such warmth that they care about you! And so, it's like a little happy family I guess you can say. So, your emotion starts developing where you start seeing that, hey, I'm not just a nobody. (Zane, incarcerated WHoS participant)

A dominant theme related to the environment of WHoS revolves around the presence of volunteer artists from the community. All the men expressed an appreciation for having volunteers come in and highlight the pivotal role they play in fostering a positive, accepting environment at WHoS. Notably, as will be explored, the men underscore how the presence of volunteers creates both a contrasting setting and contrasting social interface from what they are used to in prison.

The volunteers come into WHoS and work alongside the men throughout the workshops and productions. As community artists, the volunteers assist with a range of creative aspects such as costumes, set design, sound, and even acting. However, beyond the technical support they offer, the volunteers provide the men with the opportunity of being interacted with in an accepting, non-judgmental way. Joe speaks to this when he describes the approach and attitude the volunteers embody, "You know, they come in here and they don't give a crap who you are. You treat them right and they're going to treat you like a member of their family. And for somebody that never had that, it's big" (Joe, incarcerated WHoS participant).

Logan further elaborates on this:

> These people I mean they don't know you but they come in here and they just show you love and it's just like wow! We are blessed to have these people who come in from nowhere and all of a sudden, they're in, they're here with us in the mix and you know, there are lots of us in here doing life—I mean almost the whole main cast, we are doing life sentences—they're not scared […] and it gives you hope! When you can come into a place and [be] shown love by a complete stranger, that's pretty, it's pretty ground shaking for some people. I know a lot of people in here they never really had love, they never had acceptance—things that people assume that they probably had. (Logan, incarcerated WHoS participant)

As Joe's and Logan's words demonstrate, for many of the participants, being perceived by others without a negative overcast appears to be an uncommon experience. Coming into WHoS, the volunteers work with the men as individuals and as artists rather than seeing them as "prisoners," "offenders," or "criminals." That is, the status or label that is attributed to an individual comes to be de-emphasized through interactions with the volunteers. This appears to be because the volunteers are neither prison staff nor prisoners and thus, share a context beyond the prison walls.

The men routinely describe the volunteers as individuals from the "outside" or "from the street." Goffman's (1961) theorization around secondary adjustments whereby individuals may experience forms of freedom within the institution is relevant to this discussion. Goffman (1961) identifies sociable associations or interactions with outsiders as a way in which the inmates may partake in secondary adjustments. As Goffman (1961) describes, by interacting and having contact with members of the public, inmates can detach themselves from both their "stigmatized status" as well as the institutional culture. The experience of the men with the volunteers of WHoS can thus be understood through this conceptualization. Interactions with institutional staff are guided by the view that the men are "offenders" and are under their authority, while the inmate culture and its associated hierarchies frame the interactions that occur between the prisoners (Clemmer 1940). However, in being unaffiliated with neither the staff nor the prisoners, the volunteers offer unique interactions that are contrasting to the normalized interfaces that take place in prison. Dylan, a formerly incarcerated WHoS participant, illustrates this when he reflects on the nature of the relationship the men have with the institutional staff compared to that with the volunteers:

> There is an opposition with the correctional officers, even the correctional officers that weren't in uniform; they are still correctional officers so you can't be candid. A lot of guys open up to somebody from the street, but they can't open up to someone else—they can't say what they want because they are afraid it's going to go on their file. And if you are a lifer [serving a life sentence], that's going to be in your file forever. (Dylan, formerly incarcerated WHoS participant)

The men regularly express how the dynamics with the volunteers are less restricted and rigid while the interactions with the institutional staff are more reserved given the dynamics of power and authority of the staff. Jake further reinforces this:

> [Being able] to express yourself to somebody that's not trying to observe you and look for fault, they just look at you as a person. It's something [prison] needs more of […] You are always so guarded there, you have to watch what you say, you have to watch how you act, you have to fall within these certain parameters of behaviour, otherwise you could be shipped [transferred]. Volunteers are a huge part of it. They really are. (Jake, formerly incarcerated WHoS participant)

This echoes the findings in Goffman's *Asylums* (1961) where he observed greater ease in activities guided by individuals or "specialists" external from the institution. However, not only is the nature of interactions characteristically different, but more importantly, the men perceive these relationships as being more personable. As Brandon explains:

> Like I understand we have counselors; I have a PO [Parole Officer] […] But we're not friends, you know it's a professional relationship. So even whether it be a program facilitator—they have the

information, but it's very sterile. WHoS was a very holistic environment [...] to be able to make these connections with people is what is best for me. It's a big part of what I take away from it. (Brandon, incarcerated WHoS participant)

Apparent from the narratives of many of the men, the approach the volunteers take in working with the men entails a non-judgmental and accepting environment. Jewkes's (2005) and Crewe et al.'s (2013) conceptualizations around the fronts and façades that prisoners put on are fruitful in this context. This is precisely because it appears that with the volunteers, the men can drop the fronts they so often wear when interacting with the institutional staff or other prisoners. Several of the men spoke of how their interactions with the volunteers, particularly those who have been involved with WHoS over the course of several years, invoke trust. The volunteers get to know the men for whom they present themselves as, and their interactions are not centred on the men's offences, actions, or incarceration—as is often the case. Rather, these communications entail ordinary discussions, or otherwise those that are distant from the prison context. In a sense, the volunteers are like a window into the "outside" world where they provide the men with a sense of distance from the institutional context. This further demonstrates how the interactions with the volunteers may be understood as a secondary adjustment or intermission to the prison context (Goffman 1961). The separation between the outside world and the institution narrows with the presence of volunteers. As can be understood through Goffman (1961), the social barrier characterizing total institutions comes to be partially uplifted.

In being backstage at WHoS during our site visits, we witnessed many conversations between the men and volunteers and took part in several ourselves. These conversations ranged from topics on theatre, to more casual discussions on pop culture, to what life is like "on the outside." However, regardless of what the discussions were, it was apparent that the men at WHoS were engaged with the volunteers and members of the public. For Kevin, an incarcerated WHoS participant, the sincere and open engagements with the volunteers are immensely meaningful because, as he describes, "it's about making connections, and when you make connections like that with people, you remember that sort of stuff." For several of the men, connecting with the volunteers as a part of WHoS is particularly special given their unique background in the arts. As Dave, an incarcerated WHoS participant, expresses, "one of the things I highlight, and I highlight as really important, is the community engagement with the arts community and with the academic community as well [...] I appreciate that kind of opportunity to connect with those folks."

Apparent from the analysis, the collaboration and interactions the men experience with the WHoS volunteers allow for a sense of connectedness with the community. While the current literature on prison theatre recognizes the involvement of volunteers, artists, and theatre practitioners, the research has not highlighted the significance of their role. That is, the engagement, collaboration, and interaction that take place in these theatre initiatives with volunteers and artists have been overlooked. This may partially be because individuals who are involved in prison theatre initiatives have carried out most of the research on prison theatre themselves, which may make the identification of their position less apparent to them or otherwise more difficult to acknowledge. However, evident from all the interviews with the participants in this study, the WHoS volunteers offer an environment contrasting to the tensions that typically characterize interactions and relationships within prison. This speaks to insights drawn from Crewe et al. (2013, 69) whereby the researchers conclude that the education and chaplaincy personnel within prisons promote atmospheres and interactions that are "less prison-like." Beyond the interactions with the volunteers being unique and positive, the interviews with the former WHoS participants in this study shed light on how collaborating with the volunteers in WHoS has proven to be an invaluable learning experience.

Many of the former WHoS participants speak of how connecting with the WHoS volunteers has helped them in their reintegration now that they are in the community. This is particularly expressed in terms of how interacting with volunteers assisted them in moving away from the way they normally projected themselves in prison, which many of the men alluded to as being rather adverse and forthright. Dylan speaks to the adjustments he learned to make that come about through his interactions with WHoS volunteers:

> Things like this should be included more and should be encouraged, because you are around society [...] That's the big thing for me, WHoS broke down barriers and prison attitudes, stuff like that, because being in and out of prison all the time for the past 20 years, it's like it seeps this negativity and judgmental things that aren't congruent with becoming a productive member of society. So these things become part of your being and who you are, and

you don't really notice it because you are not around people. For the past 20 years I've been mostly around drug addicts, criminals, and prisoners, so the attitude is adjusted to that […] So being a part of WHoS was breaking that down because you have outside people coming in, you got to address them a certain way and you can't be disrespectful [because] you have people that are compassionate, and caring coming in to give their time. (Dylan, formerly incarcerated WHoS participant)

Jake's experience further speaks to how working with volunteers through WHoS resonates with him:

I learned how to communicate in a prosocial manner. [In prison] you would speak in a very forthright and blunt manner and you said what you meant and you meant what you said; and you can't do that in theatre! You have to circumvent, you have to include niceness. You have to do it with tact and coyness and it worked out really well […] And I kept thinking, "well how would I prefer to be talked to?" And again, that's through the people coming in; you don't do it—you can't speak to them like they're a convict, and you get used to that. I was in for almost 18 years and you get prison speak. So, it was nice especially since that it is a releasing institution, helping us set up to release and reintegrate into society. You know, you don't use the F word for everything—you try to not use it at all. Your vocabulary improves. (Jake, formerly incarcerated WHoS participant)

Thana's personal experience of interacting with the men at WHoS and seeing them interact with the volunteers testifies to this. All the men interacted courteously and with mutual respect with the volunteers. In fact, the men were particularly sensible with how they were speaking with anyone from the community. For example, we noticed that as the men were speaking to us, whether it was during the interviews or backstage, they would almost always apologize for their language if they happened to swear. We observed many of the men do this with the other volunteers as well; exemplifying Jake's account of how the men actively adjust their communication through their interactions with volunteers. This parallels the emerging recognition in the literature, which suggests that prison theatre may help with enhancement and development of social skills (Tocci 2007).

Figure 4.2. Artist performing alongside the men in *Sleeping Giants* (2016 production).
Source: Jam Hamidi for William Head on Stage.

Beyond the interpersonal developments and opportunities stemming from interactions with the WHoS volunteers, all the former WHoS participants express how many of the volunteers embody a support network for them in the community. Many of the men share how they keep in touch with many of the volunteers because they left such a positive impression on them at WHoS. As Armin explains:

> Ya, if it wasn't for all of these people that I met there [in WHoS], I'm not saying I'd go back [to prison], but I wouldn't be doing as well [...] A lot of people get out of prison and get back to their old ways. This kind of gave me another avenue; it's a support group. [...] If you have the right people there, it can help you. (Armin, formerly incarcerated WHoS participant)

Beyond shedding light on the fundamental role that the WHoS volunteers have in fostering positive interactions, this theme also speaks to the importance of volunteers in assisting with the reintegration of individuals back into the community. Thus, the men's testimonies regarding their interactions with the WHoS volunteers affirm how volunteers provide individuals with what CSC recognizes as a "bridge" back into the community (CSC 2017a).

4.3. Connecting Outside

> For me it's about changing the perception on what prison is like, the stereotypical inmate, whatever you want to call it. Because the public doesn't really know what goes on in prison, all they really know is what happens on TV right. So, to change their attitudes and points of view by showing them the artistic side of all of us—I think helps break down the barriers. (Kevin, incarcerated WHoS participant)

In the hour before the WHoS performance, the parking area of William Head Institution fills up, as car by car the audience starts coming in. A line is formed at the entrance of the prison as individuals sign in and pass through the security procedures. Van after van, the staff at William Head Institution drive members of the public through the landscape of William Head Institution to the Programs Building, where the WHoS experience awaits them. Part of what makes WHoS unique, which sets it apart from some of the other prison theatre initiatives around the world, is that WHoS opens its doors for the public to come in. With close to fourteen shows every year, and about one hundred seats per performance, the captivating performances of WHoS reach about 1,400 individuals every year. While it is undoubtedly an experience for members of the public to witness and to be a part of the magical performances of WHoS, let alone the experience of going into a prison, the men of WHoS hold immense value for having the public come in. A prominent theme throughout the narratives of the men is how WHoS is an opportunity for them to challenge public perceptions of prisoners and incarceration more broadly.

By having audience members come into the institution and witness the WHoS productions, the men can connect with the public and reveal sides of themselves that are more than often overshadowed by stereotypical understandings of prisoners (Pickett et al. 2013). Mainstream media outlets, including television shows and movies, are saturated with portrayals and depictions of those incarcerated as dangerous, violent, and frightening. The "othering" of those incarcerated seen in media spectacles shape perceptions and understandings of prisoners in society. The men at WHoS recognize a lack of understanding from the general public whereby they are often vilified by both society and the media because of their status as prisoners. As Rick, an incarcerated WHoS participant describes, "I know most of society are very stereotypical of inmates, of jail inmates—until it happens in their family [but] I'm not like what most of society thinks of me."

Echoing the participants' recognition of the negative perceptions present in society, there is an ever-growing acknowledgement within the criminological literature on socio-cultural understandings of crimes and "criminals"—which often represent distorted understandings perpetrated by the media (Ferrell et al. 2008; Landry 2013; Munn 2012; Paulsen 2003). However, WHoS affords the men with the unique opportunity to directly challenge mainstream understandings of prisoners by having the public come into the prison and witness their productions. Michael speaks directly to the role of WHoS in contesting the stereotypical views on prisoners: "Society believes that we are these Hollywood monsters, and we are not anything like that. And that's what I think WHoS challenges; that we're people who've made mistakes but, we're people who can create beautiful things that touch people" (Michael, incarcerated WHoS participant).

The audience is reminded to reflect on the humanity of the men and their capacity of being more than society's label of them as "offenders" or "criminals." Reinforcing Michael's account, Andrew, a formerly incarcerated WHoS participant, further speaks to the role WHoS plays in providing them with an opportunity to challenge societal views. Reflecting on his involvement with WHoS, Andrew expresses the importance of having the public be a part of WHoS experience: "Bringing the public in—there is huge risk in that. But, the reward is the public gets to come in and see people as human beings not with stripped shirts [...] It's a vehicle for a message to society [...] we have a stage, what do we want to say off that stage? And so that's our voice, let's use our voice with theatre" (Andrew, formerly incarcerated WHoS participant).

Notably, at WHoS, the audience are not passive observers. Instead, during the end of the performance, a talkback is facilitated by the WHoS community artists during which questions can be asked and interactions between the audience and the men take place. The men share many of the interactions and discussions they have with audience members during the question-and-answer period at the end of their performances. These interactions partly speak to the role WHoS may play in building connectedness and reworking societal misconceptions. As Logan, an incarcerated WHoS participant, expresses, "people have said I never thought it would be like this, or you know—I only saw stuff on TV or I never heard the stories, or the newspapers make it sound super bad." Several men share personal accounts they had with audience members as well. Kevin, in reflecting on a discussion he had with an audience member after a WHoS performance, shares how the individual appeared genuinely affected by the WHoS experience: "He goes, 'it's helped me drop the stereotypical image that I had of you guys. You guys aren't like what they show on TV.' And this is a grown ass man, an older man telling me this and he's getting emotional, and I'm just sitting there thinking, yo, we've done something good!" (Kevin, incarcerated WHoS participant).

Dave further speaks of the opportunity WHoS affords the men in challenging mainstream discourses on prisoners:

> It's an intervention on the side of the public, the citizens. I'm doing this marketing survey for the last couple of weeks and one question is "what drew you out?" —It's the experience of coming into a prison to see prisoners perform—that's usually the one that they pick. But then I follow up with another question, "what do you see are the benefits of the production?" Breaking down fear-based stereotypes of prisoners—that's the one that's usually pick [...] So I think, ok, the public comes in, maybe they're just paying $20 for some entertainment, rather than going to a movie theatre, but then afterwards they're like "ok ya, this did challenge some of my emotions of prisoners as these monsters and villains—because they're artistic, they're creative, they're vulnerable on stage." So, if it has that effect on a segment of the local community, [then] they have a more balanced understanding of prisoners afterwards. (Dave, incarcerated WHoS participant)

This theme, drawn from the men's narratives, extends Dworin's (2011) view of how performances staged by prisoners may resonate with audiences because they are personal experiences. As Dworin (2011, 101) describes, "[...] it keeps alive the possibility of a change in attitudes among people who may not have the opportunity to touch the humanity of inmates directly." The men at WHoS have a chance at re-writing the narrative around those incarcerated. Parallel to this, the audience of WHoS is also put in a context where they are exposed to the dedicated, artistic, and creative sides of the men, aspects that are not part of the mainstream image of prisoners that is reinforced by society (Ferrell et al. 2008; Landry, 2013). As Zane, an incarcerated WHoS participant puts it, "when the public comes in, they can look at prisoners as not being all over bad and not paint us all with the same brush."

Our experience of seeing the WHoS performances and witnessing the response of the audience reflects much of the accounts the participants share. As we sat in the audience, we were able to overhear some of the conversations the audience members were having. In one instance, as we were waiting to leave the institution, we overheard an audience member reflect on their experience of watching the production to their partner. Interestingly, their comment about the WHoS men was, "They seem so normal!" This observation is interesting because the audience member's reaction speaks to the potential of WHoS to challenge the conventional "othering" of prisoners in society (Ferrell et al. 2008). The impression that WHoS leaves on the audience encourages the public to think critically about their biases, as well as the broader function of the criminal justice system within our society. As Jayden, an incarcerated WHoS participant, explains, "This is not just for [the public's] $20, it's also for them to know this process is making us better people [...] We are being put in a position where we can work on ourselves, not just dress up and act in a play. It's bigger than that!"

Beyond the opportunity to contest and rework the public's conceptualizations, during the interviews the men also share how WHoS gave them an opportunity to reveal a different side of themselves to those who know them. As Kevin explains, WHoS allows the men to challenge some of the understandings of institutional staff within the prison:

> Even in the institution, staff that see you preform are like, "well we never thought of you as like that"—because all they do is read your file, and then they see [you at WHoS], and well you're doing something totally out of the norm. And you know, it's rewarding to hear staff say that they view you differently now that they've seen you do either a dance or an act or whatever right. Because it changes everyone's perception on who you are. This is a great

outlet just to do something different. (Kevin, incarcerated WHoS participant)

While a large portion of the audience are members of the public who are attending WHoS for the joy and entertainment of it, a notable portion of the audience are family and friends of the men at WHoS. At the talkback in one performance, a mother took the microphone and heartfeltly expressed how proud she is of seeing her son on stage alongside the other men. Many of the men share how their family members come in as a part of the audience to witness them involved in the WHoS production. Through this, the men express how they can also present themselves in a unique way to their loved ones. For example, Jackson shares the significance of having his mother come in and see him perform: "My family seeing me on stage—that was pretty big. My mom has never really seen me do anything with my life, so for her just to see me in that light—it was like she used to take me to see all those shows when I was a kid and for me to put on a show for my mom, it was really gratifying" (Jackson, incarcerated WHoS participant).

Kevin, an incarcerated WHoS participant, voices a similar experience when he shares the significance of having his brother come in and see him act in a WHoS production: "My brother came and watched the show […] he was crying because he goes, 'I see you in a totally different light, from where you came to what you're doing now'."

The literature on prison theatre has largely overlooked the role that such initiatives play as being a voice for the men or a means through which to challenge the public's perceptions of prisoners. Apart from select emerging research (Fesette et al. 2021; Pensalfini 2019), prison theatre scholarship has not engaged with the role that prison theatre may play as an intervention for the public. As such, the exclusivity of WHoS in having the public come in and the theme shared from the narratives of the WHoS men around public perceptions offer an interesting addition to the literature while also highlighting the uniqueness of WHoS. In turn, this speaks to imaginative criminology as it demonstrates how through prison theatre initiatives like WHoS, participants may be able to communicate and project new understandings around incarceration, which contest mainstream (mis)conceptions. As Andrew, a formerly incarcerated WHoS participant, puts it, "it doesn't work—there is nothing without the public coming in. I can go to my house and put on a puppet show—if there is no audience there, then that's all I'm doing."

Figure 4.3. Physical theatre performed in-the-round for *Chalk* (2010 production). *Source:* Jam Hamidi for William Head on Stage.

CHAPTER 5

Character Development

> *What I find it does is it gets people out of their comfort zone and they realize that if they can do something like this, there's not much that they can't do. And for some guys that's all they need, is kind of a little push to get over this hump and then they go from there.*
>
> – Joe, incarcerated WHoS participant

5.1. Overcoming Challenges

Like many of us, most of the men at WHoS have never performed on a stage in front of a live audience. By being a part of WHoS, many of the men's discussions centre on the confidence that they develop from being able to challenge themselves. This, as Joe's testimony alludes to, is often expressed with regards to the experiences facilitated by WHoS, which pushes the men out of their comfort zone. Correspondingly, the men emphasize the transformation and growth they experience from being a part of WHoS. Our discussions will explore how WHoS helps unlock the participants' capacities, skills, and self-confidence as they learn how to stretch themselves beyond their habituated engagements and experiences within prison.

The men speak of several ways that WHoS assisted them with stepping out of their comfort zone and overcoming some of their personal challenges. However, public speaking and having to perform in front of an audience are the dominant emerging narratives. Many of the men speak of the difficulty associated with having to stand on stage and present in front of others. Andre, an incarcerated WHoS participant, explains the uneasiness of his experience of having to perform in WHoS for the first time:

> I looked at the crowd, and my heart was just pounding—like out of my shirt! I thought I had a panic attack, I thought I was going to hyperventilate, pass out, fall down, fall off the stage. Ya! It was way more than I expected. I knew I was getting out of my comfort zone to do it, but I didn't expect that to happen to me […] But now, I look up to the light, pretend nobody is there and I get through it. It is getting better. I'm not as nervous, it still kind of happens but it is a lot better than the first time. (Andre, incarcerated WHoS participant)

Most of the men spoke of the difficulty of having to go up on stage and be in the spotlight. This appears to be a shared experience for most of the men, regardless of their respective roles in WHoS—be it acting, dancing, or playing in the band. Notably, many express how the first performance of WHoS is particularly difficult because aside from it being the first, this is also the production that is performed to the prison-inmate population before opening to the public. Unlike having an unknown public audience, in the first performance, the men are placing themselves in front of their acquaintances and peers—making it particularly challenging.

Several indicate that their participation in the WHoS production largely stems from their desire to challenge themselves interpersonally, as is the case for Thomas: "I had decided I wanted to do that [WHoS] mostly because I'm an introvert, don't do anything really—public speaking or anything like that. So I knew this would be very good for not just my Correctional time, but for myself—a personal goal kind of thing" (Thomas, incarcerated WHoS participant). Through their involvement with WHoS, the men are given an opportunity to directly step out of their comfort zone and work through any apprehensions they may have when it comes to performing or public speaking.

The men underscore the importance of WHoS in allowing them to challenge themselves given the prison context. Drawing on Goffman's (1961) theoretical conceptualization of total institutions, prison is characterized by administered and sanctioned rounds of life. Activities are limited and mundane given their basis on routine and formal administration (Goffman 1961). However, WHoS can be seen as a break from the structured routine given that it involves opportunities for the men to challenge themselves and engage in activities that are distinct from the normalized occurrences in prison. Accustomed to the ordinary occasions of life inside prison, WHoS gives the men the stage, literally, to engage and work through their apprehension of presenting and standing in front of others. As Michael, an incarcerated WHoS participant, reinforces, "it gets us out of our comfort zone and guys take away something that they would never get to experience—more than likely, anywhere else."

The opportunity to challenge themselves and step out of their comfort zone in WHoS translates into a narrative of personal development and growth. This is precisely because entrenched in the men's testimonies are discussions about the confidence they have developed from being able to challenge themselves. Kevin describes how significant WHoS has been in building his confidence, given that it allowed him to overcome his long-standing struggle with public speaking, which he attributes as playing a pivotal role in the problems that ultimately led him to prison:

> I believe that WHoS—if WHoS wasn't around, I would've still been struggling with my fear of public speaking. And kind of getting through that, increased my confidence, and made me believe in myself that I can overcome the internal critic. That's like huge for me right because I defeated myself half the time with my thoughts about "I can't do this, or so and so is so much better—how come they can do it and I can't?" And I used to always say that when it came to oral presentations and public speaking. I give 100% credit to WHoS, and [the artists] because they gave me the opportunity to take on a bigger role, to start challenging myself—and had it not been for this, life could've been very different [...] WHoS—out of everything within my 14 years of doing programs, this is the stuff that helped me believe in myself. (Kevin, incarcerated WHoS participant)

Kevin's testimony on WHoS echoes the experience of many of the men, who emphasize the role that WHoS plays in helping them overcome their fears and build their confidence. Having this experience and ability is particularly notable for the men given that their involvement in the criminal justice system means that they will likely need to go up in front of a parole board at some point in their sentence.

The confidence the men gain through WHoS unlocks their capacities and reassurance in themselves. For Sammy, WHoS has helped him realize his capabilities and the importance of challenging himself, which he parallels to his reintegration process:

> There is a lot in here that is capable of doing a lot. Don't have limits, there's always things that if you want to do it, you can do it, you can pull it off. It kind of breaks that fear mechanism—you don't want to live in "I can't do this" […] I can relate it to being in prison—me being in for how long I've been in, doing a life sentence and on my way out—trying to get out is not giving up. Try to better yourself and break those barriers—this kind of thing helps. It helps a lot. (Sammy, incarcerated WHoS participant)

In gaining the confidence to step out of their comfort zone, the men voice how WHoS has correspondingly inspired them to take on new challenges. Several men speak of their interest in now expanding their involvement to music, poetry, and other creative performances. The confidence developed from their involvement with WHoS enables the men to begin to redefine their understandings of their abilities. As encapsulated by Logan:

> It gives you the confidence to try something new that you've never done before. You don't want guys getting out jail angry with no hope of the future, you know. Now they really have confidence to try something else or go into this, maybe they try that, because now they have this experience where you know what, this is one of the biggest fears ever—its public speaking, and we did that, so now what can we do? (Logan, incarcerated WHoS participant)

Indeed, as the case for many of the former WHoS participants, WHoS has encouraged them to continue to seek creative opportunities outside of prison. Illustrative of this is Armin, a formerly incarcerated WHoS participant, who shares how since he has been out of prison he has been both volunteering and auditioning for theatre opportunities in the community.

Being a part of WHoS for several years, Michael describes how his favourite part about WHoS is seeing the men's confidence blossom: "Seeing the men around me grow and thinking that there is no way they can do something and then they end up doing it—and they're just shocked by their own ability. I think I take a lot of pride of guys feeling good and doing well" (Michael, incarcerated WHoS participant). The role of WHoS in assisting the men in developing confidence resonates with the findings of previous studies, which suggest the role that theatre has in building self-confidence (Merrill 2015; Moller 2003;

Tett et al. 2012; Tocci 2007). However, extending beyond this finding, the narratives of the men at WHoS reveal how, by being able to work through personal challenges and engage in new experiences, WHoS enables them to build their confidence.

It is important to note that the personal growth the men experience occurs throughout their involvement with WHoS as opposed to solely during the theatre performance. That is, for many of the men, stepping out of their comfort zone and building confidence begin before the commencement of the public performances. Rather, it is through the workshops, activities, and continuous support provided by the volunteering artists that, as Lincoln, a formerly incarcerated WHoS participant, explains, "whatever that's inside of you that's scared kind of quiets down." Facilitated by the community artists and volunteers who are involved with WHoS, the men describe the workshops that take place in the months preceding the production to be the warm-up that incrementally prepares them for the final production. It is in these workshops that the men begin to challenge themselves by singing, acting, and performing in front of each other. Seth's reflection of the men during the WHoS workshops illustrates this process when he describes the development they go through:

> Here's the funny thing. It starts off as a room with twenty-five people, and [they] are all very quiet. About a month into rehearsals, they are asking questions, saying I can do this, I can do that, I can take more dialogue. You built it from people on the fringes that are hiding in the shadows to all of a sudden, they all want to be on the stage. (Seth, formerly incarcerated WHoS participant)

For many of the men this progression took place over the course of several years being involved in WHoS. For Rick, an incarcerated WHoS participant, performing in front of an audience became easier after being involved in WHoS for several years. As he reflects, "my very first [performance], I was more nervous than an alligator in a handbag factory I'll tell you that much. But, this year, after being on stage for a few years, it's easy for me. I don't know, more of a comfort." The majority of the men shared how they often started off in WHoS, with a small role and progressively started taking on bigger roles and greater responsibilities, as they grew more comfortable.

Figure 5.1. Singing and performing live music in *The Crossroads* (2018 production). *Source:* Jam Hamidi for William Head on Stage.

For a lot of the men, joining WHoS is in and of itself an endeavour that is out of their comfort zone. Several of the men speak of their initial reluctance in joining WHoS. Much of these accounts can be understood through the masculine ideals characterizing the prison culture (Ricciardelli 2015; Ricciardelli 2014a). Participating in theatre can be seen as being in contrast to the hyper-masculine, intensified version of manhood that is generally upheld in prisons. As Michael's words suggest, "How many men in the community would wear sequins, glitter, and everything else, and embrace everything that WHoS does in a very male driven environment? How many men in the community would even think about doing that? Not many!" (Michael, incarcerated WHoS participant).

Theatre offsets the robustness, toughness, and hyper-masculine aura of prison. Many of the men describe how they did not initially think of themselves as "the theatre type" because they would normally spend their leisure time playing sports or exercising—activities which align with hegemonic masculine ideals (Connell 1995). Despite this, the men express their sincere gratefulness for stepping out of their comfort zone and getting involved with WHoS. As Armin asserts, "It was something I would never do, but I am so glad I did."

5.2. Unlocking Capacities

Importantly, stepping out of their comfort zone and being involved in WHoS has permitted the men to also develop and practise many of their skills. The men often express how WHoS puts them in a context where they can apply the skills they have learned through various programs and interventions. Further to this, because WHoS is an inmate-run theatre company, the men also speak of how they are able to put to work many of their technical skills, such as carpentry, sewing, electrical work, and music. In discussing this, the men repeatedly point to how WHoS provides them with a real-life atmosphere that is different from the normative sequences of prison.

Several of the men share how they have been enrolled in various correctional programs and interventions throughout their incarceration. In these programs, which are offered through the institutions, the men express how they are taught a range of skills and tools related to self-management, personal standards, and emotional regulation. However, given the prison context and environment, several of the men note how they are not able to apply much of the knowledge and skills they develop. As Andrew expresses, "there are only so many programs [in prison] — courses I guess they're called and then go sit in your room for 15 years. Well, what do you do? All the other things were just like social groups — sit in a meeting room" (formerly incarcerated WHoS participant). As can be understood through Goffman's (1961) notion of total institutions, the routinized and arranged environment of prison does not permit the men to overtly practise or engage with many of the skills they are acquiring. Interestingly, the narratives of the men reveal how WHoS offers a "real world" atmosphere and unique opportunity for the men to apply their knowledge and transferable skills. Jayden speaks directly to this:

> It emulates real world atmosphere. Because there are certain jobs here where you would work with a civilian, but that's like your only interaction. Here, you get guys that don't deal with their emotions properly, that's a big reason of why we're all here, we didn't deal with certain things properly and it kind of went to other areas of our life. So, I think that would be the key of just, you know, putting us in a real world setting and having us to deal with certain things while coming together. I mean, you're not going to

find a job where you're always going to get along with your boss, or along with the whole group of staff […] I think its good practice. (Jayden, incarcerated WHoS participant)

In a discussion that parallels Jayden's words, Jackson also speaks of the opportunity that WHoS provides the men:

I think the thing that makes it [WHoS] different is that you're putting yourself in real life situations—you're actually being tested with all the skills that you learn in programs; they teach you how to deal with conflict, how to manage your emotions, things like that. And then when you're in WHoS you're actually using those skills—like you have to because there are all kinds of personalities there and you don't know what you're going to get. (Jackson, incarcerated WHoS participant)

Importantly, the opportunities available in prison for the men to use or apply their skills are often limited (Goffman 1961). Speaking of his involvement with WHoS, Lincoln, a formerly incarcerated WHoS participant, shares: "I wanted something to really push my artistic vision and side because that was so limitedly tested in previous years in prison—I just never had an avenue for that." As an inmate-run initiative, WHoS challenges the men to come together and work with each other. That is, WHoS places the men in situations where they are both enabled and challenged to directly apply their skills. The men describe this feature of WHoS as being a distinguishable element, as mainstream happenings in prison do not permit such rich opportunities. As Karl puts it:

Programs are more academic, where there are tools that they introduce to me, and WHoS is the opportunity to practise some of those skills…it's a good learning experience. Just—you meet new people, you see new challenges, things that I need to work on with people, like conflict resolution skills and anger, and my personal standards—all that. (Karl, incarcerated WHoS participant)

The autonomy WHoS maintains as an inmate-run theatre company translates into the men being involved in every stage of the theatre devising project. For example, Jake's background and experience in carpentry led him to get heavily involved in set designing and the building aspects of WHoS. Others share how WHoS allows them to directly apply and utilize some of the technical skills they learned while in prison. Exemplary of this is Karl, who when speaking of his involvement in WHoS shares: "I was supposed to do the lights, because I was taking an electrician course, so I figured it was good practice" (Karl, incarcerated WHoS participant). Similarly, Joe shares how he can use his sewing skills and abilities that he learned in prison by getting involved in creating costumes for the production. As he explains: "Well see, I've been in prison for thirty-two years now and my first job in prison was in the sewing shop. So, I learned how to use the sewing machine, the serge, cut material, how to put patterns and do all that. So, that's where I learned it, and then I just kept it" (Joe, incarcerated WHoS participant). Thus, being an inmate-run initiative, the theatre company evidently provides ample opportunities for the men to apply many of their technical skills, much of which are artistically driven.

The combined efforts and talents of the men spread across the different aspects of the theatre company integrate into the development of a professional and captivating production put together by the men. The lighting, music, costumes, set, and all the other design aspects of the production encompass an abundance of detail and creative elements. Notably, costumes in every production put on by WHoS are intricate and capture the spirit of the characters. Intricate in design, the costumes worn by the men often include sequins, beading, textured layers, as well as personalized masks, headpieces, and props—all of which are made by the men. Additionally, the comments from the audience during the question-and-answer period more than often express surprise at how everything is done by the participating prisoner—whether it is the music, costumes, or the set. As Sammy puts it, during his reflection on one of the previous WHoS productions:

> There are a lot of talented guys so the show actually was pretty successful—because the coordination and then how everything flowed, there was a couple of singers that were really talented singers and musicians, and the costumes were really good, the lighting and everything—for a prison play it was like, wow. It was pretty good! Even people that were like "what the fuck are you guys doing here? What the hell is this?"—they come to watch it and they are blown away because it's not what they expect. (Sammy, incarcerated WHoS participant)

WHoS being an opportunity for the application and practising of skills appears to be a novel addition to the current literature on prison theatre. The research considering prison theatre has conceptualized the role that these initiatives play on skill development, particularly interpersonal skills (Moller 2003; Tocci 2007; Tett et al. 2012). However, prison theatre has yet to be understood as offering an opportunity for the men to also apply their skills. As encapsulated by Kevin, an incarcerated WHoS participant, "this was an opportunity for me to use my skills in a more productive manner […] an avenue for me to put it to good work."

CHAPTER 6

Revising the Script

For these guys to have that opportunity to do something that they wouldn't normally do, and then have the Q & A at the end, or have people clap for them, that's a self-esteem booster—and sometimes people in here need that because they haven't had much to look forward too.

– Jayden, incarcerated WHoS participant

6.1. Changing the Monologue

A further emerging theme related to the environment of WHoS pertains to the men's development of self-esteem and self-worth through their involvement with the theatre company. There are several key features that are characteristic of WHoS that the men speak of that are conducive to fostering their self-esteem, self-worth, and more broadly, their sense of accomplishment. As will be explored, the presence of supportive audience members and volunteers plays a particularly significant role in promoting these with the men of WHoS.

Throughout the interviews, the men speak of the significance of having an audience and members of the public come in to watch their shows and support the work of the theatre company. This is often discussed in terms of the standing ovations and positive, supportive comments that are received at the end of almost every WHoS performance. All the men express how the engagement and gratitude shown by the audience leave positive impressions on them. For Andre, he expresses how the best part of the whole production is seeing the audience's response:

> I think that my most enjoyable part of the performance is that standing ovation at the end—like I just feel so proud of myself and for everybody that I work with, like how much hard work. Because it was hard, it was a lot of hours, a lot of time spent here working on it, and then having everybody just really voice their emotion at the end of it with the standing ovation, standing up and clapping—and then speaking to us after in the Question and Answer period and telling us how much they enjoyed it, I think that's the best part about it. Ya, it makes me feel really good! Like we really accomplished something. (Andre, incarcerated WHoS participant)

The men who are involved with WHoS put in a lot of time, effort, commitment, and collaboration to put on a production each year. As all the men emphasized, the production entails months of preparation and often full days dedicated to putting different elements together. Given this, witnessing and feeling the audience's positive response to their efforts bolsters the participants' self-esteem and, more importantly, their sense of accomplishment. Demonstrating this, Jackson expresses how:

> It's a trip when I think about it now, because this has been my life for the past—I don't know, five to six months. But now, when I take a step back and look [...] It's so rewarding, it makes me feel like I've accomplished something. Like just to see the crowd, and when we get the ovations, and they're standing, and the comments we get at the end; it's like really fulfilling. (Jackson, incarcerated WHoS participant)

Beyond giving them a sense of achievement, the participants' narratives reveal that the positive feedback received from the audience is particularly meaningful because it is a response and reaction that they are not normalized to receiving, given their criminalized status and the prison context. Many of the participants share how they internally struggle with viewing themselves in a positive light. Brandon speaks to this in reflecting on his situation and the role WHoS has played in the development of his self-esteem:

> I've been in for a long time and it's hard to get up every day for why I'm in prison, and still look myself in the mirror and say, "I'm a pretty good person." Most men are going to get out of here feeling really shitty about themselves. That's just a fact, that's just how it is. Most men get out of here and they do not have any self-esteem. We may be a little cocky, even bordering on arrogant, but in our inner—we really don't feel very good about ourselves [...] And I think that this, the WHoS, really is a step forward in the right direction. It really is. I've never in my entire life received that much positive affirmation and feedback for anything I have ever done. (Brandon, incarcerated WHoS participant)

Brandon's testimony, which is reflective of a shared experience expressed by many of the men, is one that can be understood through Goffman's (1961) theorization of the mortification of the self in total institutions. The process of being incarcerated, particularly over an extended time, involves the curtailment of one's sense of self. As Goffman (1961, 4) describes, "here one begins to learn about the limited extent to which a conception of oneself can be sustained [...]" However, WHoS, particularly the reception of the positive engagement from the audience, may be understood as a form of secondary adjustment given that it offers the participants both an experience and gratification that they may not otherwise attain in the normative prison setting. As Dave, an incarcerated WHoS participant, explains, "I think for a large degree there is some egotism going on that kind of motivates and pulls guys to WHoS—and I include myself in that." In particular, having individuals from the public and local community come in and show support is extremely resonating for the men. As is exemplified by Logan's account:

> People, in these places and myself included, have gone through times where we have low self-esteem or low self-worth. So, when people compliment you, you sometimes doubt the authenticity of it. You would be like okay, well they're just trying to be nice. But, when you see over a hundred people standing up, clapping and

cheering, you're like "okay this must have been good!" (Logan, incarcerated WHoS participant)

Despite the men's sincere expressions of appreciation and gratitude for having the audience's support, several participants speak of the difficulty in accepting such positive feedback. It was not easy for some of the men to accept many of the compliments and affirmations they receive because it is a response they are not used to in prison. As Jackson, an incarcerated WHoS participant, explains, "we don't really get much you're doing a good job, this and that—they point out the things you're doing wrong." Michael's account speaks further to this:

> Being in Corrections I think we always hear the negatives, and its reinforced over and over again, the things we've done wrong, what's not right about us, you know things we need to work on. But, at some point, there has got to be some positive there. I have a parole officer who is supportive but I mean, as you've been in for so many years, every piece of paper you get is cut and paste or there is a version of something negative there. (Michael, incarcerated WHoS participant)

The men are accustomed to having the focus often placed on the aspects of themselves that need improving or changing. Given this, a significant number of the participants express how it was difficult to accept any positive responses or compliments from others, whether it is the volunteers, staff, or audience. For example, Andrew speaks to his experience with WHoS where he describes how he was never able to take a compliment because he did not feel worthy. However, throughout his involvement with WHoS, he learned to be more receptive and accepting of congratulatory remarks and more importantly, to believe in himself:

> So the play would be over and everyone says "great play," "you did a wonderful job!," "you did that?," "it was so good!" and I wouldn't take credit for it; well the director told me to stand there and he did a good job too. And so I would actually avoid going out. But, I learned over time to accept them; "well thank you, yes I did do a good job, thanks ya I really appreciate it." (Andrew, formerly incarcerated WHoS participant)

The positive feedback and response associated with WHoS aids the men in reconfiguring their view of themselves. Michael expresses a similar experience where his realization and acceptance of his abilities in design only came about through his involvement with WHoS where he learned to better internalize and accept positive feedback:

> When somebody says the costumes are really good, my automatic response is "but only if you knew I didn't know how to use a sewing machine, and I didn't know how to do this" — I was like trying to talk them down from what they were saying — I second guess what I am hearing people say. So, I'm trying not to do that, I'm trying to live in the joy of what's going on now and the pride [...] I'm just learning to say thank you — and it's like I could have a future in this. (Michael, incarcerated WHoS participant)

In addition to the role WHoS plays in aiding the men with developing self-esteem and self-worth, beyond this, participating in WHoS affords the men with a sense of fulfillment. Throughout the interviews, the men indicate that their involvement with WHoS is an avenue for them to engage in a positive initiative, or as many describe it, a "prosocial activity." Jackson speaks to this when he reflects on his involvement with the theatre company:

> I really don't have much real-world experience, like I was sixteen when I came in so I didn't really live a life, so just knowing that I'm capable of doing more is gratifying. And seeing the looks on people's faces and you know, just hearing from you, it makes me feel like I'm doing the right thing, and I've never felt like I've been doing the right thing before. (Jackson, incarcerated WHoS participant)

Notwithstanding the presence of a wide range of activities, programs, and support groups, there is a limited number of initiatives within the prisons that appear to provide the men with a sense of fulfillment where they feel they are contributing to something bigger than themselves. In being able to put on a show for the public to enjoy, many of the men perceive WHoS as a way to give back to the community. As emphasized by Lincoln:

You know, this was an opportunity for us to give to our community, let's be real. That's exactly what it is. Never done that before […] My outside community—I had only ever taken from them […] So every now and then, you watch the rows [in the audience] and you appreciate these people, and you know you're doing it for them and I got a chance to really look at them. We made people cry, we made people laugh, we made people stand and applaud. And it felt amazing. (Lincoln, formerly incarcerated WHoS participant)

Extending beyond the performances that WHoS put on for the public, WHoS donates a fraction of their revenue in ticket sales to a charitable organization. This philanthropic feature of the theatre company is an aspect that is meaningful to the men as it is a way they can further contribute to the community in a positive way. For Samuel, an incarcerated WHoS participant, "being a part of that process really makes us feel like we are doing something positive for the population and for the community."

The enhancement in the men's self-esteem and self-worth parallels findings from Tett et al. (2012) and Brewster (2010). While both research studies suggested that art-based initiatives play a role in the enhancement of the participants' self-esteem, these studies do not provide nuanced understandings for prison theatre as both studies examine broader art-based programs. Furthermore, the research within the literature does not reveal what specific qualities or aspects of these programs particularly lead to an enhancement in the participants' self-esteem. Drawing on the men's narratives and experiences with WHoS, this research not only further demonstrates the role that prison theatre may play in building self-esteem, but it uncovers how the positive and supportive environment of WHoS promotes this development in the men. In particular, the analysis reveals how it is the positive reception the men receive for their efforts in the theatre company that cascades into the development of elevated self-esteem. In the prison context where an individual's sense of self is constantly contested, faults are often focused upon, and opportunities to contribute to the community are limited, WHoS becomes instrumental in uplifting the participants' self-esteem and the recognition of their self-worth.

Figure 6.1. The men performing as a part of *Here: A Captive Odyssey* (2015 production).
Source: Jam Hamidi for William Head on Stage.

6.2. Performing Agency

> We are self sustaining, and I think that's the grassroots feature of [WHoS] it's a self-initiative we sustain as prisoners [...] it gives us independence because it's not a program, it's not an intervention — it's voluntary. (Dave, incarcerated WHoS participant)

A dominant theme emerging from the men relates to how WHoS is an opportunity for them to express their agency, or otherwise assert their independence. As Dave's words allude to, the men often describe this with regards to WHoS being both a voluntary leisure activity and an inmate-run initiative. Together, these features appear to allow the men's involvement in the theatre company to represent a means for standing apart from the institution and the confines associated with incarceration. This theme will be explored through Goffman's (1961) theorization of total institutions where prison may be understood as a context where the expression of agency and independence is both limited and often compromised.

While interpreted diversely within the social sciences, agency may be viewed as, "the ability for individuals to express their power and act independently from the constraints of social structure" (Calhoun 2002). However, the overall regimented environment within prisons limits the degree in which self-determination, autonomy, and freedom of action can be exercised. WHoS, in being an inmate-run initiative, allows the men to express their agency, or otherwise assert their independence through their involvement. In line with his symbolic interactionism approach, Goffman (1959) conceives the self as arising from the various social interactions and arrangements of life. However, in total institutions and immediately upon entrance, one is stripped away from these social arrangements and interactions. Traces of the identities of inmates are also scrutinized by various procedures and practices, such as through the issuing of identification numbers or confiscation of personal items. The separation of the inmate with the wider world coupled with abasing procedures that assault the inmates' sense of self and self-worth mark the beginning of curtailment, or what Goffman (1961) deems as the mortification of the self. There is the continuous and constant prescription, judgment, and sanctioning of a person's line of behaviour. In turn, inmates are limited in their capacity to act independently or otherwise express their agency.

As the theatre company is operated by the men themselves, many speak of a sense of ownership, responsibility, and autonomy from the institution. While some of the participants sit on the board where they are responsible for the administrative aspects of the production, such as budgeting and advertisement, others are responsible for putting together the design aspects, such as set, costumes, and props. In doing so, Dave, an incarcerated WHoS participant, stresses how WHoS is, "ultimately an opportunity to highlight our productivity in a creative way that is not totally guided by the institution." This may be understood as being particularly prominent given that it is less common for institutions to have initiatives that are operated by prisoners. Most of the programs and interventions offered in prisons are either run through CSC or through community support groups and volunteers. However, as WHoS is an inmate-run initiative, the men come to be actively engaged in all aspects of the theatre company, making their involvement extend beyond being passive participants. In this respect, Andrew's words are demonstrative of this when he considers the uniqueness of WHoS:

> All the other things were just like social groups, sit in a meeting room. This [WHoS] was a business that was run by the inmates

[...] Ya it is still a self-run business [...] complete responsibility of it. If you screw it up really bad one way or another, there might not be one next year. So there was nothing close to it. (Andrew, formerly incarcerated WHoS participant)

As Andrew's words illustrate, WHoS gives the men an opportunity to be engaged and immersed in a unique way where the theatre company is actively run by them.

As WHoS is an initiative that does not operate as a correctional program under the broader guise of rehabilitation, the men tend to be further drawn to partaking in the theatre company. Dave, an incarcerated WHoS participant, speaks directly to this when he reflects on the operation of WHoS: "The public comes in and actually purchases a ticket to watch us, so it's like a small business enterprise rather than a program intervention, so that's like important because we are technically doing it for drawing a crowd to kind of sustain ourselves over time." This resonates with Shailor (2011) who, in his book on prison theatre, also suggests that the significance of these practices stems largely from their fundamental feature of not having their purpose explicitly mandated to instill change.

The expression of agency and independence that WHoS affords the men can be further conceptualized by Goffman's (1961) theorization of secondary adjustments within total institutions. Secondary adjustments allow inmates to experience some measure of autonomy and exemplify ways in which individuals may stand apart from the institution (Goffman 1961). While WHoS operates under institutional oversight and parameters, the theatre company is autonomous from the institution and thus, may be understood as a form of secondary adjustment. As Kevin expresses:

When you got a company that's owned by the inmates [...] you don't want to lose that—because this is for us, this is about us, this is about our ability to express ourselves in a manner that we don't have through programming or talking to our POs [Parole Officers] [...] I think if it was like CSC program a lot of people wouldn't want to be involved. (Kevin, incarcerated WHoS participant)

Kevin's account of WHoS reflects those shared by many of the participants. Several of the men in the interviews express how their interest in getting involved in WHoS largely stems from the initiative being inmate run. Operating in this way, there appears to be an alleviation of scrutiny felt by the men in comparison to their experiences in other programs and practices within prison. As Joe explains, "[At WHoS] you can say what you want; you don't have to be afraid of anything going on paper. The worst fear of anybody doing time is somebody writing stuff down on paper. There's a fear of that because it happens so much" (Joe, incarcerated WHoS participant).

Like Joe, many of the men express how they experience less discomfort in WHoS than they do in other programs and activities because their behaviour is not being overtly sanctioned. As the men's accounts demonstrate, WHoS would likely not bear the same significance for the men if it were a program offered and operated completely by the institution. In his conceptualization, Goffman (1961) asserts that secondary adjustments do not function to introduce radical change to the existing institutional structures, but rather they may often avert actions that may be seen as disruptive. As is the case for WHoS, the theatre company does not operate to radically alter institutional structures. Instead, it is through their ability to express their autonomy from the institution that WHoS may be understood as being a form of secondary adjustment that subliminally allows for resistance against underlying structures. As Joe puts it, "even though it's controlled quite a bit, we have to realize where we're at and the restrictions. But, the fact that we're allowed to create and just go, ya it's big!" (Joe, incarcerated WHoS participant).

The men note how the leisurely aspect of WHoS sets it apart from many of the programs offered in prison. That is, the men's involvement in the theatre company is not mandated or compulsory. Rather, participating in WHoS is optional and the level of involvement the individual accepts is also up to the participant to decide. For example, many of the men speak of deciding to only get involved in the workshops and the behind-the-scenes aspects of WHoS, while others choose to audition and be involved in the acting aspects of the production. Unlike the dominant environment of prison where activities, tasks, and programs are often prescribed to the prisoners (Goffman 1961), getting involved with WHoS is a decision the men make themselves. As Jake, a formerly incarcerated WHoS participant, describes, "It's not a program. It's a volunteer thing. This is my leisure time." In expressing this, the men regularly describe the limited autonomy they have in the prison context.

The men's narratives are further demonstrative of Goffman's (1961) notion of the mortification of the self whereby the vast majority of one's behaviour in total institutions are constantly prescribed and sanctioned. Similarly, Clemmer (1940) also perceives how prisonization, or the socialization process into the inmate culture, creates personal disruptions for the inmates as they begin to assume the passivity attached with their role as inmates (Gillespie 2002). Armin, a formerly incarcerated WHoS participant, speaks to this when he shares how in prison, he views programs as "forced." Aside from required programs, other aspects of the prisoners' lives are often controlled through the institution, which further limits the degree to which personal autonomy and self-determination can be exercised. As Goffman (1961) asserts, these restrictions, which, outside of total institutions are performed through one's personal autonomy, are demonstrative of how inmates further experience a mortification of the self. In the context where personal autonomy is constrained, the participants' narratives reveal how their involvement with WHoS can be understood as a break or counteractive feature to prison. That is, for many of the men like Brandon, participating in WHoS holds meaning because it stems from their self-determination and own personal desire to get involved:

> I think what it comes down to is I don't have a lot to be dedicated to in here, or that I want to be dedicated to. And this is an opportunity for the men and myself to put as much effort as I want into. And WHoS was an opportunity for me to be involved in that way, to put in a ton of hours and effort because it felt important. (Brandon, incarcerated WHoS participant)

WHoS being an opportunity for the men to express their agency appears to be a novel theme to the literature on prison theatre. The literature has predominately focused on prison theatre programs that are operated either by the institution itself or by support groups. Given this, the theme of expressing agency and autonomy is not highlighted in the existing research on prison theatre. As it currently stands, there does not appear to be a prison theatre initiative like WHoS functioning as a theatre company operated and sustained by the inmates.

Figure 6.2. The men on stage in *The Crossroads* (2018 production). *Source:* Jam Hamidi for William Head on Stage.

CHAPTER 7

Curtain Call

Throughout this book, we have aimed to highlight the experiences of the men with WHoS in order to gain an understanding of the impact this theatre initiative has on their lives. By way of our work, our desire is to produce text and research that is reflective of the men's voices and experiences while capturing the rich aspects of WHoS. Through the narratives of the incarcerated WHoS participants and former WHoS participants, we shed light on the significance of WHoS and the role that theatre plays within the correctional context. Notably, we wanted to go beyond simply recounting the experiences of the men; rather we have tried to understand them, particularly within the structural and social context of prison. As criminologists, we sought to expand the scope of the current literature by implementing a conceptual framework that encapsulates the prison structural and social context. Resonating throughout the analysis of the men's experiences, this book unravels how the impacts of prison theatre are largely rooted in the contrasting nature of these arts-based initiatives to both the prison structural and social context (Goffman 1961; Sykes 1958).

In conducting this in-depth research on WHoS, we intended to expand the literature on prison theatre initiatives and more specifically, extended the discussion on prison theatre to a Canadian context. Despite the success and resilience of WHoS operating for over four decades, this theatre initiative has gone largely unrecognized in the academic literature. It was not until we started this work that we quickly learned that what underlies this absence of WHoS is likely the caution in certain moments to have WHoS and the work done by the men be misconstrued. That is, throughout Canada's history, there have been waves of "tough on crime" agendas and ideologies that could have threatened the operation of WHoS. Thus, this likely led the desire to protect and preserve the creative work that the men do at William Head Institution, keeping it largely in the shadows. Evident from the narratives shared and presented throughout this book, WHoS is precious for all those involved, from the men to the artists and prison administrators, to even the local community. However, through this book and the testimonies presented from the participants, we shed light on WHoS in a way that helps substantiate it as Canada's long-standing, inmate-run prison theatre initiative. As Jayden, an incarcerated WHoS participant, shares in reflecting on our research, "I would hope that this reaches the right eyes to give others the opportunity to not only do this, but also see the positives that come from WHoS." Indeed, we hope this is achieved through this book.

With much of the knowledge on prison theatre stemming from anecdotal evidence, we wanted to conduct research that can tease apart the impacts of prison theatre on the lives of criminalized individuals. In exploring WHoS, the current study responds to limited knowledge within the literature regarding both the relevance and impact of prison theatre initiatives (Hughes 2005; McAvinchey 2011; Merrill 2015; Tocci 2007). By conducting interviews and attending to the experiences of current and former participants of WHoS, we bring the narratives and testimonies of men into both the discourse on prison theatre and the criminological research more broadly. This feature offers a significant contribution to the literature as the perspective of criminalized populations have been largely overlooked (Brown 2008).

Within criminology and particularly from a correctional perspective, there is often an emphasis on offender rehabilitation and the delivery of structured interventions. We did not approach this research to investigate the capacity of WHoS in this sense, as WHoS intrinsically operates as an inmate-run theatre company. However, through our examination of WHoS and analysis of the narratives and experiences of the men, we come to learn that WHoS, though not a traditional, structured intervention, aligns with discourses around desistance, preparation for release, and rehabilitation. WHoS offers opportunities for the men to re-imagine themselves, grow as individuals, develop skills, form connections and support networks, and express their sense of agency. That is, the overall WHoS experience as well as the commitment, work, and effort the men put towards this theatre company fosters what within the criminological literature is understood as protective factors, or positive circumstances, and influences that support a pro-social lifestyle (Serin et al. 2010). This is reflected by the camaraderie WHoS supports, the emotional expression it permits, the connection with the community, as well as the sense of independence it offers the men.

Importantly, the merit of WHoS goes beyond considering its alignment with post-release and desistance paradigms. Many of the insights and themes that emerged from the men would likely be lost or otherwise overlooked if prison theatre was viewed strictly through such an approach. Notably, from the perspective and experiences of the men, our analysis point to the significance of WHoS in assisting and supporting men through their incarceration. WHoS and its associated theatre devising work opens the door for new opportunities and capabilities for those who are incarcerated. Further to this, the narratives suggest that through the presence and engagement of a public audience, WHoS provides the men with opportunities to challenge societal views and (mis)conceptions around those incarcerated. With the fundamental nature of prisons representing a separation between society and those behind the walls, this opportunity that is enabled through WHoS stands as particularly impactful. Academically, this helps anchor the significance and relevance of creative arts, such as theatre within criminology and prison settings. By exploring an arts-based theatre initiative, this study responds to the growing call of imaginative criminology to adopt more creative areas of inquiry that expand the field's milieu (Carlen 2016; Frauley 2015; Jacobsen 2014; Young 2011).

Taken together, by highlighting and making sense of the experiences of the men with WHoS, we hope that this book serves as a connecting point that resonates with everyone—correctional administrators, criminologists, artists and theatre practitioners, scholars, students, and even those incarcerated. Having operated for over four decades through the efforts of the men, the guidance of artists, the provision of the administration at William Head Institution, and the support of the community, we hope that the creative creations of WHoS continue to grow, with a future longer than its history. We leave the reader with the words of Michael, an incarcerated WHoS participant, who eloquently reflects on the power of WHoS:

> At the end of the day WHoS has survived because there are people who really enjoy it, not just in here but out there. It's unique, and WHoS gives of itself more than we give it, it just keeps on giving. Yes it's draining, yes it's time consuming, it costs money, but at the end of the day it gives more than it takes—and it's a win-win. It's a win for the guys in here, it's a win for the staff, it's a win for the public, it's a win for the arts community—it just continues to grow. (Michael, incarcerated WHoS participant)

Appendix A

Literature

In considering the research on prison theatre, much of the literature stems from the discipline of applied theatre and is often undertaken by art practitioners who have worked within prison theatre programs (Balfour et al. 2019; McAvinchey 2011; Moller 2013; Pensalfini 2016; Prendergast 2016; Prendergast 2013; Shailor 2011; Thompson 1998; Tocci 2007). While the research is scarce and limited, there have been different approaches used within the literature examining the implications of prison theatre. Generally, research on theatre programs in prison often focuses on one of two areas: the broad, societal impacts of these initiatives, and the individual impacts. Research looking at the societal impacts of prison theatre is often evaluating the effectiveness or usefulness of operating these arts-based initiatives. As such, studies considering societal impacts often involve investigating the contribution of these initiatives to correctional objectives, often through quantitative methodologies. In turn, this body of research seeks to examine the recidivism or reoffending rates of individuals involved in theatre programs or, alternatively, conduct cost-benefit analyses on these initiatives (Cheliotis and Jordanoska 2016; Hughes 2005).

One of the most extensive and early studies examining societal impacts of prison theatre is from 1987 and was undertaken by the California Department of Corrections. This recidivism study investigated parole outcomes for prisoners enrolled in the Arts-In-Corrections program (AIC), an initiative that engages prisoners with an array of artistic mediums, including visual art, music, and theatre. In this study, 177 parolees who participated in the AIC program for at least six months were compared to parolees who were not enrolled in the program (California Department of Correction 1987). Parolees who participated in the AIC program were observed to have more favourable outcomes than those not enrolled in the program. AIC participants reoffended at a significantly reduced rate, compared to parolees who did not participate in the AIC. More specifically, within the first year of release, 74.2 percent of AIC participants maintained a clean record compared with only 49.6 percent of non-AIC parolees (California Department of Correction 1987). Despite the promising conclusions drawn from this study, examining the AIC program, which offers an assortment of arts-based activities, yields limited understanding on the contributions of prison theatre. As Day (2019) describes, while there are different rationalizations for operating arts-based initiatives in prison, more robust evaluations of outcomes are needed from arts practitioners who situate their work within the philosophy of corrections. That is, more articulation is needed on how participating in arts programs in prison may contribute to rehabilitation or otherwise may have a meaningful influence on the broader crime desistance process. While arts practitioners may be cautious to reduce the inherent value of their work in a way that speaks to correctional and rehabilitative perspectives, Day (2019) emphasizes the need for more clarity in this regard for correctional accreditation and endorsement.

A particularly noteworthy study that sheds some light on the rehabilitative potential of theatre in prison is a 1998 study led by Stephen Duguid of Simon Fraser University. This report consisted of an extensive investigation of the Prison Education Program, which operated from 1973 to 1993 in federal institutions across British Columbia. Through this program, various liberal arts courses were offered to prisoners as well as extracurricular activities, which—of particular relevance to this book—included a theatre production group. In this three-year research study, Duguid (1998) followed 654 released prisoners who participated in the education program, with the primary objective of examining whether the education program is effective in reducing the rate of recidivism. While the study focuses on prison education, a subsection of this multifaceted research project looked specifically at the theatre production group sponsored by the universities, which ran adjacent to the education program. This subsection of Duguid's (1998) study bears particular relevance given that the theatre program examined represents the initiative that in later years evolved into WHoS. By looking at cases, Duguid (1998) found that individuals who participated in the theatre program had a better post-release success rate (55 percent) than their predicted post-release success, as determined by their Statistical Information on Recidivism Scale score (SIR; 36 percent).

Notwithstanding the findings from Duguid (1998), these correctional-driven studies only yield partial understandings. Given the complexity of criminal behaviour, it is uncertain whether or not participating in the theatre initiatives has a direct bearing on post-release behaviour. That is, though prison theatre may contribute to desistance from crime (Davey et al. 2015), considering the post-release behaviour of individuals who were involved in prison theatre may be seen as reductionist. In turn, and alternative to this approach, several studies have considered looking at the costs and benefits of operating arts-based programs in prisons.

To understand the broad societal implications of arts-based programs, a number of studies have relied on cost-benefit analyses (Brewster 1983; Johnson et al. 2011). Evaluating societal impacts of arts-based programs through quantitative cost-benefit analyses are noteworthy because they contribute to the field in a unique way. As addressed by McAvinchy (2011), studies applying quantitative approaches present anecdotal evidence in numerical and statistical forms that speaks to policymakers, criminal justice administrators, as well as anyone apprehensive about the financial expenses of operating arts-based programs. In this regard, the Arts Alliance in the United Kingdom commissioned a report to explore the value of arts in criminal justice settings through an economic analysis (Johnson et al. 2011). Johnson et al. (2011) considered the costs and benefits of arts-based programs in the rehabilitation of criminalized populations. This report examines three arts-based programs, which include the Clean Break Theatre Company, Only Connect, and Unitas. All three programs demonstrated to be economically beneficial, given reductions in reoffending. For example, Johnson et al. (2011) estimate that for the women's theatre company Clean Break, for every £1 invested in the program, there is a £4.57 value yielded for society, over one year. Similar cost savings for the criminal justice system were determined for the other arts-based programs examined. This echoes earlier findings from Brewster (1983) which examined the AIC Program offered by the California Department of Corrections in four different institutions. In this early evaluation, the economic cost for the social benefits of the program were quantified and weighed against the economic cost of delivering the program. Through the financial model of considering social return on investment, Brewster (1983) showed the AIC program as being a cost-effective initiative.

Albeit their contribution to the field, studies examining the societal impacts of theatre initiatives have been challenged in the literature given their positivist underpinning (Balfour and Poole in Thompson 1998; Thompson 2009). As reinforced by Hughes (2005, 37), "methods for assessing cost effectiveness are complex and contested, and many impacts of the arts are difficult to quantify, especially in terms of monetary return." These studies tend to reduce a multi-dimensional area of inquiry into numerical data guided by quantitative, evaluation-based discourses. Prison theatre programs and practitioners may subscribe to the dominant evaluation discourse of measuring and quantifying their work in order to prove their legitimacy. In this regard, there is greater support in the literature for the use of qualitative research approaches given that they are more harmonious and in line with the intrinsic nature of arts-based initiatives (Balfour and Poole in Thompson 1998; Brewster 2010; Merrill 2015).

In looking at societal impacts of prison theatre beyond positivist approaches, emerging research has begun considering the role of prison theatre performances on society. Drawing on his extensive involvement with Prison Shakespeare, Pensalfini (2019) sheds light on the ways in which theatre performances not only impact the participants involved, but the audiences as well. As Pensalfini (2019) describes, prison theatre audiences enter with the knowledge that they are seeing a performance by actors who are incarcerated and have been found guilty of an offence. As such, witnessing performances of prison theatre, such as Prison Shakespeare, offers a personable connection that may trigger shifts in preconceived understandings and perceptions of those who are incarcerated. This is reinforced by more recent work done by Fesette et al. (2021) on the Phoenix Players Theatre Group (PPTG) in the United States with regards to having spectators from the community. In examining the performances put on by the PPTG, Fesette et al. (2021, 474) note how they, "[…] extend the public vision beyond the notions of prison life constructed and regulated by the carceral state." Parallel to this, in her exploration of prison theatre and theories of desistance from crime, Davey (2019) posits that public performances done through prison theatre initiatives offer a shift in how incarcerated or criminalized individuals are seen by others. That is, prison theatre performances offer a form of connection that serves as a form of mediation or reparation between those who are incarcerated and the community.

While the emerging research on prison theatre has considered the societal impacts, the research has largely focused on the contributions of these programs on the participants themselves (Branders 2023; Hughes 2005; Merrill 2015; Pensalfini 2016; Tocci 2007). As it will be explored, the research looking at the individual impacts of prison theatre tends to take on the form of qualitative case studies. A common theme emerging from the prison theatre literature considering the individual impacts relates to confidence building. For example, based on a case study conducted on the Clean Break Theatre Company, a theatre program for women, Merrill and Frigon (2015) investigated the transformative power of theatre for criminalized populations. Through the exploration of emerging themes, Merrill and Frigon (2015) examined the role of transformation and growth for participants enrolled in the theatre company. Notably, the participants in this study indicate how their involvement with Clean Break helped build their confidence. From overcoming fears, to being given the opportunity to overcome feelings of rejection or isolation, theatre engagement helped the participants gain confidence through the theatre creative process (Merrill and Frigon 2015).

Other case studies on prison theatre have shed light on the significance of these initiatives on the participants. In the book *The Proscenium Cage*, Tocci (2007) conducts a series of case studies in the United States on three prison theatre programs: Theatre for the Forgotten, Cell Block Theatre, and Prison Performing Arts. Tocci (2007) highlights how prisoners were able to engage in appreciated and purposeful behaviour, which participants share allowed them to feel respected. Furthermore, Tocci (2007) suggests that the unique emphasis of theatre on interaction and socialization distinguishes it from other arts-based programs in prison, which tend to be more individualistic. Prisoners described theatre as providing them with an avenue to express themselves and a means for self-discovery and self-evaluation. In line with the expression of the self, Fesette et al. (2021) extend these findings through their recent examination of The Phoenix Players Theatre Group (PPTG) operating at the Auburn Correctional Facility in New York. Through the techniques and practices employed by PPTG, including the use of rasabox exercises, Fesette et al. (2021) note how the men can engage and embody their emotions. Through their participation with PPTG, the men are given the opportunity to recognize their full humanity and allow themselves to fully be seen. In turn, Fesette et al. (2021) highlight how PPTG offers a space that operates against the visual regime of control observed in the carceral space. The potential of prison theatre initiatives to develop practical skills amongst participants is a prevalent theme within the literature. Notably, emerging case studies have showcased the pivotal role theatre plays in allowing participants to develop social skills. A group of case studies conducted by Tett, Anderson, McNeill, Overy, and Sparks (2012) on prisoners participating in arts-based intervention programs in Scottish prisons explored how these initiatives help foster social skills, specifically collaboration, amongst participants. In particular, these arts-based programs centred on music, opera, and theatre. The analyses from Tett et al. (2012) found that arts-based programs help enable collaboration between the prisoners. The programs created opportunities for the prisoners to work collectively and establish a sense of trust, which Tett et al. (2012) indicate as enabling the participants' to further build their self-esteem. As the researchers describe, "all the projects involved people in working together so that the more withdrawn participants were brought out of their shell," (Tett et al. 2012, 178). By collaborating as a team, the programs allowed the participating prisoners to connect and support each other.

Through the collaborative and supportive environment offered by the programs, participants were encouraged and motivated to improve their verbal and written literacy skills. Parallel with Tett et al. (2012), similar observations in terms of literary skill development is shown in research on the Shakespeare Prison Project (SPP; Bates 2003; Pensalfini 2019; Pensalfini 2016; Shailor 2011). SPP is a prison education program that allows prisoners to engage in studying, rehearsing, as well as performing Shakespearian plays. Participating prisoners in this program showed greater interest in engaging with both education and literature (Bates 2003; Pensalfini 2016). Notwithstanding the presence of these studies, there is an evident gap in the literature looking at the experiences with prison theatre and the impact it has on those participating, particularly from a criminological perspective. Recent emerging scholarship within the prison theatre literature has engaged in more theoretical considerations of prison theatre (Branders 2023). In her research looking at artistic interventions within Bapaume Detention Centre and Vendin-le-Vieil Central Prison in France, Stathopoulos (2023) offers valuable insight into the transformative power of theatre. Notably, in her focus on participant observations and interviews, Stathopoulos (2023) points to how, as an experience, art and theatre challenge the prison system and its associated social dynamics. In prison, where expression and individuation are limited, artistic interventions allow participants to counterbalance these confining experiences and develop new socializations. This echoes the earlier work of Siganos (2008) in her book *L'action culturelle en prison : Pour une redéfinition du sens de la peine*. Siganos (2008) points to the importance of cultural activities within institutions, such as prison theatre. For Siganos (2008), these activities can reveal the possibilities of correcting the repressive nature of the prison environment. While incarcerated individuals are faced with dehumanization processes and limitations of prison, Siganos (2008) asserts that creative, cultural activities may be regarded as empowering efforts to combat the negative effects of incarceration. Theatre thus allows those who are incarcerated to restore their senses through artistic expression and, therefore, may be seen as playing a role in the reintegration process.

Similarly, Woodland and Hazou (2021) reorient the literature on prison theatre to one where art and prison theatre are perceived as a form of resistance to state-sponsored control over individuals. That is, in being under prison confinement and control, Woodland and Hazou (2021) highlight the capacity of prison theatre to challenge the system and enhance the freedom and liberty of those involved. A similar theme emerges from Hazou and Daniels' (2022) autoethnographic work examining a creative project in New Zealand and the United States. By engaging in the theatre workshops and creative work, Hazou and Daniels (2022) suggest that participants can engage with concepts of oppression and liberation and ultimately, unshackle their body, mind, and spirit from the context of incarceration.

Appendix B

WHoS Productions and Projects

Date	Productions and Projects
Spring 1981	The Birthday Party
Fall 1981	Dracula
Spring 1982	The Knight of the Burning Pestle
Fall 1982	Ten Little Indians
Spring 1983	Macbeth
Fall 1983	One Flew Over the Cuckoo's Nest
Spring 1984	The Paper Cage
Fall 1984	Stalag 17
Spring 1985	Fools
Fall 1985	Born Yesterday
Spring 1986	Wait Until Dark
Fall 1986	The Dancing Mice
Spring 1987	See How They Run
Fall 1987	The Mad Dog Blues
Spring 1988	Don't Drink the Water
Fall 1988	Curse of the Starving Class
Spring 1989	Hamlet II
Fall 1989	My Three Angels
Spring 1990	The Odd Couple
Fall 1990	Rosencrantz and Guildenstern Are Dead
Spring 1991	Early One Evening at the Rainbow Bar & Grill
Fall 1991	The Stranger
Fall 1992	Beyond Mozambique & Leftover Crumbs

Spring 1993	*Fathers*
Fall 1993	*The Boys Next Door*
Spring 1994	*Marat / Sade*
Fall 1994	*Right Bed, Wrong Husband*
Spring 1995	*The Bacchae*
Fall 1995	*Amateurs*
Spring 1996	*No Exit & Endgame*
Fall 1996	*Our Country's Good*
Spring 1997	*Mr. 80%*
Fall 1997	*Bathroom Humor*
Spring 1998	*Ripe Conditions*
Fall 1998	*One Flew Over the Cuckoo's Nest*
Spring 1999	*Andromeda & The Waiting Room*
Fall 1999	*Three Penny Opera*
Spring 2000	*No Room for Love*
Fall 2000	*Criminals in Love*
Fall 2001	*Playboy of the Western World*
Spring 2002	*The Cage & The Tell-Tale Heart*
Fall 2003	*The Elephant Man*
Fall 2004	*The Firebugs*
Fall 2005	*Autobahn*
Fall 2006	*Macbeth*
Spring 2008	*Waiting for Godot*
Fall 2008	*Animal Farm*
Fall 2009	*Frankenstein in Oblivion*
Fall 2010	*Chalk*
Fall 2011	*Gormenghast*
Fall 2012	*The Hobbit*
Fall 2013	*Fractured Fables: The Prison Puppet Project*
Fall 2014	*Time Waits for No One*
Fall 2015	*Here: A Captive Odyssey*
Fall 2016	*Sleeping Giants*
Fall 2017	*Antigone*

Fall 2018	*The Crossroads: A Prison Cabaret*
Fall 2019	*The Emerald City Project*
Spring 2021	*Dark Traveler* (Podcast)
Spring 2022	*Prison Theatre Time Machine* (Gallery and Mini-Performance)
Fall 2023	*Eavesdrop Café*
Fall 2024	*Hatched*

Appendix C

Methodological Considerations

With the interest in understanding the impact of prison theatre on the lives of criminalized individuals, and as an exploratory case study on Canada's only inmate-run prison theatre, this research involved nuanced methodological approaches and considerations. This section provides an overview of the methodology used for our research. First, we begin by examining the underlying notion of voice and unfold the various facets of the data collection process by presenting the study population, outlining the recruitment procedures, as well as detailing the interview process and site visit to WHoS. Subsequently, we highlight the analysis process by explicating the approach and techniques used to make sense of the data, followed by a discussion on ethics.

With the figure of criminalized individuals used throughout this research, it is important to specify the definition of this term and clarify why we have chosen to use it. In the context of this book, we use "criminalized individuals" to describe those who are in conflict with the law and have experience of being incarcerated. More specifically, this conceptualization captures the participants in this study, which include incarcerated WHoS participants and former WHoS participants who are no longer incarcerated. Rather than adopting the dominant discourse of describing this population as "criminals" or "offenders," we have explicitly chosen to describe the participants as criminalized individuals. Adopting this terminology acknowledges the social processes and describes the state they are in, rather than what they have done. In doing so, we are in turn safeguarding against the use of labels that are embedded with connotations that may stigmatize or otherwise marginalize the participants (Link and Phelan 2001; Pickett et al. 2013). As a research study involving participants who are criminalized, utilizing qualitative approaches are particularly useful when it comes to recognizing the voices and experiences of those who are marginalized (Kincheloe and McLarsen 2005; Kobayashi 2001).

Recruitment

As a case study on WHoS looking at the context of prison theatre in Canada, we engaged in purposive sampling whereby we recruited individuals who either are, or were, involved with WHoS. Purposive sampling is a non-random sample whereby the researcher requires a specific target population, given the nature or objectives of the study (Bachman and Schutt 2007; Neuman 2009). Given that one group in this study encompasses incarcerated individuals (inmates/prisoners) and the other group encompasses individuals who are in the community (former inmates/prisoners), we used different recruitment methods for each group.

For the incarcerated WHoS participants, the recruitment process took place during Thana's site visit to William Head Institution. We began with Thana meeting with the WHoS board members[1] first to introduce ourselves and the research study. This meeting was essential for establishing a connection with WHoS and having them be a part of the research process. This initial interaction with the WHoS board enabled us to learn more about the dynamics and general operation of WHoS. During this meeting, the WHoS board members were provided with the recruitment forms to distribute amongst all WHoS participants. It was important to us that the recruitment process was done through the WHoS board members rather than through administration or staff at the institution. Accordingly, we did not want participants to view us or the research as being a part of the institution and correctional system, nor did we want participation to be perceived as obligatory—which would be in contrast to voluntary and informed consent.

In addition to this recruitment process, participants were also recruited in-person throughout Thana's extended and frequent visits to William Head Institution. Thana was able to regularly be present at the institution, particularly in the Programs Building where WHoS operates. In the time spent there, Thana talked to many of the men of WHoS and invited them to participate in the study. As the men got to see and meet Thana, there was a growing interest in participating given the rapport that was developed. Many approached Thana

---

[1] The WHoS board comprised three members, all of whom are prisoners.

and expressed their interest in participating in an interview because they were encouraged to participate in this study by others who had taken part in an interview. With this, it is important to recognize that snowball sampling also occurred whereby those who participated in an interview referred others to take part in the study (Atkinson and Flint 2001; Bachman and Schutt 2007).

The recruitment of former participants of WHoS was approached differently given that these men are no longer at William Head Institution, nor are they incarcerated. To facilitate the recruitment process for the former WHoS participants, we reached out to a community artist who has collaborated with WHoS for several years and has directed productions for the theatre company. This artist played an instrumental role in the recruitment process of this group given that she was able to reach out and connect us with both former WHoS participants, as well as other artists who are in contact with former WHoS participants. A recruitment, introductory email invitation was sent to the artist for distribution to the former WHoS participants. Individuals interested in participating contacted us directly via email or phone to express their interest in participating, or upon their request, had the connecting artist forward their contact information to us. In both participant groups, referrals and support for participation from the WHoS board members or community artists aided in the establishment of our approachability and legitimacy with the men.

The Interview Process

The data-collection process for this study took place in October of 2017, during Thana's visit to Victoria, British Columbia and site visit to WHoS at William Head Institution. The interviews with the participants were conducted in-person, as this permits more nuanced interactions and connections to be made. With the interviews being semi-structured, questions were asked related to the experience of the participants with WHoS, while leaving room for more open-ended, flexible discussions to take place (Balfour and Poole 1998; Van Den Hoonard 2012). In preparation for the interviews, material on interviewing prisoners and interviewing men was reviewed, such as Schwalbe and Wolkomir (2003). In addition, Thana consulted with both a registered psychotherapist, as well as Sylvie's experience in working with incarcerated individuals for tips on conducting individual interviews. Interviews ranged between thirty minutes and ninety minutes, with the average length of an interview lasting approximately forty-eight minutes.

The interviews centred on the men's experiences and involvement with the theatre company. Interview guides were developed; one for the current WHoS participants and one for the former WHoS participants. Rather than a strict guide that is to be followed, the interview guides were merely created as a reference for relevant topics or questions. Interestingly, the men appeared happy to share their experiences with WHoS and many of the questions were not asked because participants would often touch on them or answer the question through their discussion during the course of the interview. With the focus of the study being on WHoS, no questions were asked about the participants' offences. The interviews instead centred on the men's experiences and involvement with the theatre company. In view of this, a nondirective method or approach to interviewing was embraced (Rogers 1945). In adopting this nondirective technique, it remained open to the direction in which the participant was going in during the interview. This meant that the dominant voice and the dialogue were coming from the men, rather than from us. Our position in the interviews can thus be seen as what Rogers (1945) describes as a "verbal mirror" whereby the responses were often either a mere reflection or clarification of the participant's responses. Doing this and adopting the nondirective approach also allowed for a better understanding and constant check and confirmation of the men's narratives (Berg and Lune 2006; Rogers 1945).

Prior to the commencement of an interview, the purpose of the study was reviewed with the participants as well as the consent form. Alongside this, it was of particular importance that it was reiterated to each participant that our research is affiliated with the University of Ottawa, rather than the Correctional Service of Canada. Participants were informed that they may skip on answering any of the questions and that they are also able to withdraw or end the interview at any point, without any repercussions.[2] Following this clarification, informed consent was obtained from the participants, which included permission to have the interview audio recorded. As part of the process of informed consent, participants were all advised and made aware that the data for this research may be used for publications. Participants

---

2   None of the participants withdrew from the study or asked for their interview to be terminated.

were assured that the interview would not be accessed or heard by anyone other than by the researchers and that any identifying information disclosed would not be released. Two copies of the consent form were signed in each interview, one for the participant and one for us.

All the interviews with the incarcerated WHoS participants took place in an office in the Programs Building at William Head Institution. We recognize that the interview context plays a role in setting the tone for the interactions and discussions that take place during the interview. For this reason, the office was arranged so that the desk was against the side of the wall, leaving no barrier between the participants' seat and Thana. This in turn helped foster more of a direct connection and a relaxed, informal atmosphere, which mirrors Rogers' (1945) non-directive, non-authoritative approach.

Unlike the interviews with the incarcerated WHoS participants, the interviews with the former WHoS participants were not confined to a specific setting. As such, all these interviews took place at local coffee shops in Victoria, British Columbia. The specific location was agreed upon during the arrangement of the interview with the former WHoS participant.

In general, the participants were very open to sharing and talking about their experiences with WHoS during the interviews. For the former WHoS participants, a factor that may have contributed to this rapport is that we connected with them through community artists that they know and that they have worked closely with in previous years. As for the incarcerated WHoS participants, rapport was established through Thana's regular presence at William Head Institution and the frequent interactions with the men from being on site for the interviews and also backstage at WHoS. When Thana would have a few minutes to spare between the scheduled interviews with the incarcerated WHoS participants, individuals often stopped by the office if they happened to be walking by. As one individual mentioned, she had become a "friendly familiar face" in the institution. All the men at WHoS, even those who did not participate in the study, were very embracing of this presence amongst them and were appreciative of any assistance offered during the backstage processes. Evidently, the men treated Thana with the same respect and kindness they showed to the other volunteers who were present backstage. Among the many aspects and tasks of the backstage processes, Thana found herself helping out and taking part in the warm-up routines, make-up application, and even the costume preparations prior to the public performances. Overall, being backstage and immersing herself with the WHoS processes helped both the participants and Thana in becoming more familiar and comfortable with each other. This in turn helped foster strong rapport with the participants as well as an overall positive research experience (Van den Hoonaard 2012).

As widely documented in the literature, researchers conducting fieldwork, particularly in a prison setting, may often feel apprehensive about being perceived as an "outsider" by participants (Schlosser 2008). Prior to meeting any of the participants in this study, we found ourselves having this same concern since we did not know if individuals would be interested in participating in the study, nor did we know how open they would be in sharing their experiences with us. However, the men of WHoS were not only very open to sharing their experiences during the interviews, but all the interactions we had with the participants were very positive. With our research being academic and notably external to CSC, the men likely felt more comfortable sharing their experience with us as the research is not affiliated with the system or incarcerating body (Schlosser 2008). Correspondingly, with the focus of this research study on WHoS, many of the men expressed sincere appreciation for us recognizing and conducting research on WHoS and, importantly, our desire and interest in learning about it through them. As Rick, an incarcerated WHoS participant, mentioned during the end of his interview with Thana:

> I'm just very appreciative of everyone coming in, such as yourself, because—I'm sure you've been told it from other cast members and so forth with the WHoS—you coming in all the way from Ottawa and doing interviews, and the study, and the research; all I can say is it's not only appreciated but, I really do hope you have a bright future in whatever you do, because you're very genuine, and that's rare—in this place anyway. (Rick, incarcerated WHoS participant)

Extending beyond how we anchor ourselves in the research study, reflexive practice in research entails that we assess how we present ourselves to the participants and how we are, in turn, perceived by them (Presser 2004). Throughout the interviews, we recognized that our identity markers, particularly as women, are in stark contrast to the participants'. However, as in the case of Bucerius (2013, 717) in her ethnographic work on male groups involved in illicit activities, Thana quickly learned that being a woman conducting research with men and in a men's prison was "[…] not a liability to overcome." Instead, our identity marker may have allowed for more expansive connections to be made with the participants and enabled more points of access (Arendell 1997; Bucerius 2013; Scully and Marolla 1984). For example, many of the participants engaged in deep disclosure during the interviews where they felt comfortable enough to not only share their thoughts, but also share their feelings and emotions. Several participants got emotional when discussing the impact that WHoS had on their lives or when reminiscing about their experience with the theatre company. We suspect that such emotional anecdotes and expressions would not have been displayed to the same degree with male researchers. That is, the differences between the participants and ourselves were not necessarily impediments or barriers to the research process (Bucerius 2013). Instead, these differences are merely aspects that we needed to be reflexive of since they may be shaping the participants' disclosure of information.

Site Visit to WHoS

Thana's site visit to WHoS at William Head Institution warrants consideration as it represents the contextual and observational aspect of this research. The visits to WHoS extended beyond merely carrying out the interviews, as during the visits Thana was able to both observe and take part in some of the processes and activities of WHoS. With the permission of the staff at William Head Institution and support from the WHoS participants, Thana was able to join WHoS during the pre-show preparations for five of the performances. Of those five performances, Thana was able to remain backstage during the course of three shows and watch the performance among the audience for two shows.

With the opportunity to go backstage, Thana was able to observe the general environment of WHoS and immerse herself in the process by taking part in some of the activities, such as make-up application, costume preparation, and warm-up routines. In being backstage, Thana did not request anything from the participants as this opportunity was meant to better understand how WHoS functions, how the participants engage in the theatre process, and also as an opportunity for building rapport with the participants. As Michael, an incarcerated WHoS participant, mentioned during his interview after Thana had been backstage for one of the shows, "I think the best thing for you, was doing what you did on the weekend, getting behind the scenes and seeing how it all works."

After each of my site visits to WHoS and presence backstage, field notes were conducted, describing the general atmosphere, the proceedings that occurred, as well as personal thoughts or reflections. While my observations and involvement with WHoS form part of the "data corpus" in this book, it is the individual interviews that form the primary analysis (Braun and Clarke 2006, 5).

Data Analysis

To facilitate the data analysis process, there were some preliminary steps that had to be taken first, mainly the transcription of the interviews from audio-speech to text. We transcribed all the interviews by listening to the audio files and typing out the interviews verbatim, including any pauses, laughter, "umms" and any other paralinguistic elements that would provide context to the participants' words (Gray 2003; Poland 1995). During the transcription process, all names were replaced with pseudonyms and the interviews were anonymized so that any information that might identify the participants was either altered or removed. Given that the process of transcribing requires frequent pauses and rewinds, we listened through each interview once prior to having it transcribed, in order to become familiar with the data. This first level of reading was valuable for permitting us to obtain a sense of the narratives shared and the experience of the participants with WHoS.

By transcribing the interviews, we were then able to thematically analyze them. A thematic analysis is the systematic approach to the examination and interpretation of data in order to identify reoccurring themes (Braun and Clarke 2006; Braun and Clarke 2013). Given the qualitative nature of this study, a thematic analysis was most fitting given its ability to highlight significant themes and concepts for understanding both the experiences of the participants with prison theatre as well as the impact that it has on their lives. Furthermore, thematic analyses allow for the consideration of latent and underlying ideas within the data (Braun and Clarke 2006). In the context of this research, it was anticipated that the impact of prison theatre may not always be explicitly or directly disclosed by the participants. Instead, the impact of WHoS may be implied through the participants' experiences and engagement with the theatre company.

The thematic analysis of the interviews was principally done inductively or from a bottom-up approach whereby themes were derived from the data (Braun and Clarke 2006). In adopting this approach to the analysis, there was no pre-existing coding frame developed for the analysis. Rather, we allowed the themes to develop from the narratives of the participants and from what was shared in the interviews. Approaching the analysis inductively was suitable given the exploratory nature of this study—particularly since the research on the impact of prison theatre is limited, and in the case of Canada, virtually nonexistent. While the thematic analysis is largely inductive, Braun and Clarke (2006) identify that researchers can never entirely free themselves from their theoretical and epistemological underpinnings, and that all research includes deductive elements within it. Data analysis does not occur in a vacuum nor do we, as the criminological researchers, enter the study with a blank slate. Demonstrably, prior to the commencement of the analysis, we were aware that some themes might likely emerge from the data, such as the development of confidence due to our familiarity with the literature on prison theatre and observations of WHoS.

The process of thematically analyzing data often starts during the data collection stage when the researcher starts to notice patterns in the data. During the time of the interviews, we noticed reoccurring themes being raised by the men. As we picked up on these themes, we made sure to take note of them throughout the process since, as Braun and Clarke (2006, 15) note, "[…] writing should begin in phase one, with the jotting down of ideas and potential coding schemes, and continue right through the entire coding/analysis process." The preliminary notes and the notes taken during the interviews act as a reference point when coding the data. To code, each interview transcript was read line-by-line to form meaningful units (or codes) for different topics, ideas, and concepts that were discussed by the participants. We coded the interviews inclusively whereby the coded excerpts were often several sentences long, in order to not lose the context in which they are expressed (Bryman 2001 as cited in Braun and Clark 2006). In keeping with the inductive approach, we coded interview data even if it did not directly relate to the major research question. This coding process resulted in an abundant number of codes, which we then collated into potential themes (Braun and Clarke 2006).

During this phase of the analysis, we organized the codes into overarching potential themes by combining codes that were conceptually related. Codes were mainly joint if they had shared or cross-referenced interview excerpts. For instance, some of the potential themes either did not have enough supporting data or they were similar to some of the other potential themes (Braun and Clarke 2006). Given this, the themes were arranged into major-organizing themes and sub-themes. The resulting themes were assessed in two tiers: first, we ensured that the themes corresponded with the coded extracts and, second, that they were reflective of the overall interview data (Patton 1990 as cited in Braun and Clarke 2006). In abiding by these considerations, we were able to ensure that the analysis and the themes conveyed the experiences of the men and captured the impacts of prison theatre in a way that is reflective of how it was shared during the interviews.

Ethical Reflections

Ethical considerations and undertakings are necessary aspects of all research, particularly that which involves human participants. With this research involving criminalized populations, particularly incarcerated and formally incarcerated individuals, we engaged in extensive ethical procedures, considerations, and precautions throughout the various stages of this research study (Guillemin and Gillam 2004; Israel 2004; Van den Hoonaard 2012). We recognize that criminalized individuals represent a population that is not only often stigmatized and marginalized in society, but also a population that is associated with vulnerable circumstances.[3] Given this and the need to gain access to a federal institution in order to interview incarcerated WHoS participants, we navigated through a complex and elongated maze of applications, submissions, and approval processes in order to carry out this research study.

In accordance with the guidelines and standards set out by the Tri-Council Policy Statement 2 (TCPS2), which guides ethical conduct of research involving humans, we prepared an extensive ethics application and approval for this research was received by the University of Ottawa's Social Sciences and Humanities Research Ethics Board (REB). Prior to

---

3   As defined by the Tri-Council Policy Statement 2 (2022, 9), "Vulnerability is often caused by limited decision-making capacity, or limited access to social goods, such as rights, opportunities and power. Individuals or groups in vulnerable circumstances have historically included children, the elderly, women, prisoners, those with mental health issues and those with diminished capacity for self-determination."

the obtaining of full ethics approval, conditional ethics approval was initially granted given that our research study on WHoS also required approval from the Correctional Service Canada (CSC). With preliminary support and interest from senior management team at William Head Institution, a comprehensive External Research Application package was submitted to CSC's Research Branch at National Headquarters. In accordance with CSC's Commissioner's Directive-009 (2017b), research external to CSC must undergo this review process whereby the proposed research is assessed on a range of criteria. This research study was granted approval by CSC, following which the accompanying security applications, clearances, and authorizations required for both carrying out this study and gaining institutional access were also all approved. As criminologists, we recognize that navigating through the maze of required approvals only represents the formal, procedural ethics needed to carry out this research study (Waldrop 2004). Beyond this, there are also underlying ethical principles and precautions that we were mindful of through this project.

As Guillemin and Gillam (2004, 273) maintain, "[…] ethical research is much more than research that has gained approval of a research ethics committee." As discussed earlier, detailing the nature of this study and obtaining the informed and voluntary consent of all the participants was emphasized prior to the commencement of each interview. This, along with the review of information regarding the participants' confidentiality and anonymity, were fundamental for engaging in ethically sound research. Further to this, and to avoid any potential feelings or experiences of exclusion, the decision was made to interview all those who were interested in taking part in the study. Doing this led to a larger than anticipated sample size, particularly with respect to the number of incarcerated WHoS participants. While we felt that data saturation had been reached, it was decided to accept all those who were interested in being interviewed. This was principally done as it was important for us to engage in ethical practice and ensure that we heard from all those who were interested in participating and did not exclude individuals.

As a way of further remaining ethically cognizant as a researcher, participants were only asked questions in the interviews that related to their involvement with WHoS. As has been mentioned earlier, we refrained from asking anything about the participants' personal information or even their "criminal history." In line with this, we did not view the participants in this study as "sources of data" (Pittaway,

Bartolomei, and Hugman 2010, 231). That is, even after having completed all the interviews with the incarcerated WHoS participants, Thana accepted the invitation of helping in the WHoS productions and decided that she would continue attending and helping out with the backstage processes of the WHoS performances. This was important because the relationship between the participants and Thana did not simply end as soon as the data had been collected. Rather, there was a bond formed between the participants and ourselves, and so it was both personally and ethically imperative that we extend her presence beyond the scope of the interviews themselves.

Intrinsically related to the underlying notions of ethics, when presenting the participants' quotes in the analysis section, we deliberately chose to present them in their contextual entirety rather than in short fragments. This is precisely to safeguard against losing the participants' voices or speaking "for" them (Alcoff 2009). Despite doing this, throughout the research study we were troubled with the idea that we may potentially be "using" the participants' voices—as is often done in research (Bruckert 2014). This concern stems from our commitment to engage in ethical research that does not exploit the participants. However, our unease in relation to this was somewhat alleviated by the fact that so many of the participants saw value in this project, were interested in participating, and were, overall, eager to have WHoS recognized in research.

References

Alasuutari, Pertti. 1995. *Researching Culture: Qualitative Method and Cultural Studies*. London: Sage Publications.

Alcoff, L. M. 2009. "The Problem of Speaking for Others." In *Voice in Qualitative Inquiry*, edited by Alecia Jackson and Lisa Mazzei, 117–136. New York: Routledge.

Andrews, Donald. 1989. "Recidivism is Predictable and can be Influenced: Using Risk Assessments to Reduce Recidivism." *Forum on Corrections Research* 1 (2): 11–18.

Andrews, Donald, and James Bonta. 2010. *The Psychology of Criminal Conduct*. 5th ed. New Providence: Matthew Bender.

Arendell, Terry. 1997. "Reflections on the Researcher-researched Relationship: A Woman Interviewing Men." *Qualitative Sociology* 20: 341–368.

Atkinson, Rowland, and John Flint. 2001. "Accessing Hidden and Hard-to-Reach Populations: Snowball Research Strategies." *Social Research Update* 33 (1): 1–4.

Attride-Stirling, Jennifer. 2001. "Thematic Networks: An Analytic Tool for Qualitative Research." *Qualitative Research* 1 (3): 385–405.

Bachman, Ronet, and Russell K. Schutt. 2013. *The Practice of Research in Criminology and Criminal Justice*. California: Sage.

Bailin, Sharon. 1993. "Theatre, Drama Education and the Role of the Aesthetic." *Journal of Curriculum Studies* 25 (5): 423–432.

Baim, Clarke, Sally Brookes, and Alun Mountford, eds. 2002. *Geese Theatre Handbook: Drama with Offenders and People at Risk*. Winchester: Waterside Press.

Balfour, Michael, Brydie-Leigh Bartleet, Linda Davey, John Rynne, and Huib Schippers, eds. 2019. *Performing Arts in Prisons: Creative Perspectives*. Bristol: Intellect Books.

Balfour, Michael, and Lindsey Poole. 1998. "Evaluating Theatre in Prisons and Probation." In *Prison Theatre: Perspectives and Practices*, edited by James Thompson, 217–230. London: Jessica Kingsley Publishers.

Bandyopadhyay, Mahuya. 2006. "Competing Masculinities in a Prison." *Men and Masculinities* 9 (2): 186–203.

Bates, Laura. 2003. "The Uses of Shakespeare in Criminal Rehabilitation: Testing the Limits of Universality." In *Shakespeare Matters: History, Teaching, Performance*, edited by Lloyd Davis, 151–163. Newark: University of Delaware Press.

Berg, Bruce, and Howard Lune. 2006. "A Dramaturgical Look at Interviewing." In *Qualitative Research Methods for the Social Sciences*. Boston: Pearson Education Inc.

Bourdieu, Pierre, and Terry Eagleton. 1992. "Doxa and Common Life." *New Left Review* 191 (1): 111–121.

Branders, Chloé. 2023. "Theatre in Prison: Towards a Subversive Stance in Criminology." In *The Emerald International Handbook of Activist Criminology*, edited by Victoria Canning, Greg Martin, and Steve Tombs, 171–186. Leeds: Emerald Publishing Limited.

Branders, Chloé. 2020. "Jouer-déjouer : Une Posture d'intervention subversive en prison." *Champ Pénal/Penal Field* 21.

Branders, Chloé. 2018. « Je suis Détenu ». Les expressions subversives des comédiens incarcérés. *Revue Interdisciplinaire d'études Juridiques* 80 (1): 93–116.

Braun, Virginia, and Victoria Clarke. 2013. *Successful Qualitative Research: A Practical Guide for Beginners*. Thousand Oaks: Sage.

Braun, Virginia, and Victoria Clarke. 2006. "Using Thematic Analysis in Psychology." *Qualitative Research in Psychology* 3 (2): 77–101.

Brewster, Lawrence. 2010. "A Qualitative Study of the California Arts-in-Corrections Program." San Francisco: University of San Francisco.

Brewster, Lawrence. 1983. "An Evaluation of the Arts-in-Corrections Program of the California Department of Corrections." *Williams James Association* and *California Department of Corrections*. https://www.ojp.gov/ncjrs/virtual-library/abstracts/evaluation-arts-corrections-program-california-department

Britton, Dana M. 2003. *At Work in the Iron Cage: The Prison as Gendered Organization*. New York: New York University Press.

Brown, David. 2008. "Giving Voice: The Prisoner and Discursive Citizenship." In *The Critical Criminology Companion*, edited by Thalia Antony and Chris Cunneen, 228–239. Annandale: Hawkins Press.

Brown, Judith. 1996. *The I in Science: Training to Utilize Subjectivity in Research*. Boston: Scandinavian University Press.

Bruckert, Chris. 2014. "Activist Academic Whore: Negotiating the Fractured Otherness Abyss." In *Demarginalized Voices: Commitment, Emotion, and Action in Qualitative Research*, edited by Kilty Jennifer, Maritza Felices-Luna, and Sheryl Fabian, 306–325. Vancouver: University of British Columbia Press.

Bucerius, Sandra Meike. 2013. "Becoming a 'Trusted Outsider': Gender, Ethnicity, and Inequality in Ethnographic Research." *Journal of Contemporary Ethnography* 42 (6): 690–721.

Calhoun, Craig, ed. 2002. *Dictionary of the Social Sciences*. Oxford, New York: Oxford University Press, 2002.

California State Department of Corrections. 1987. "Arts In-Corrections Research Synopsis on Parole Outcomes for Participants Paroled December 1980–February 1987." Santa Cruz: William James Association Prison Arts Program.

Carceral, K. C. 2003. *Behind a Convict's Eyes: Doing Time in a Modern Prison*. California: Cengage Learning.

Carlen, Pat. 2016. "Doing Imaginative Criminology." In *Liquid Criminology: Doing Imaginative Criminological Research*, edited by Michael Hviid Jacobsen and Sandra Walklate, 17–30. New York: Routledge.

Carlen, Pat. 2005. "Imprisonment and the Penal Body Politic: The Cancer of Disciplinary Governance." In *The Effects of Imprisonment*, edited by Liebling Alison and Shadd Maruna, 421–441. New York: Routledge.

Cheliotis, Leonidas, and Aleksandra Jordanoska. 2016. "The Arts of Desistance: Assessing the Role of Arts-based Programmes in Reducing Reoffending." *The Howard Journal of Crime and Justice* 55 (1): 25–41.

Clemmer, Donald. 1940. *The Prison Community*. New York: Rinehart.

Connell, R. W. 1995. *Masculinities*. Los Angeles: University of California Press.

Connell, R. W. 1987. *Gender and Power: Society, the Person and Sexual Politics*. Cambridge: Polity Press.

Connell, R. W., and James W. Messerschmidt. 2005. "Hegemonic Masculinity: Rethinking the Concept." *Gender & Society* 19 (6): 829–859.

Correctional Service Canada. 2016. *Commissioner's Directive 760: Social Programs and Leisure Activities*. Ottawa, Ontario. www.csc-scc.gc.ca/acts-and-regulations/760-cd-eng.shtml

Correctional Service Canada. 2017a. "Volunteers." Correctional Service of Canada. Last modified May 1, 2023. https://www.csc-scc.gc.ca/volunteers/index-eng.shtml

Correctional Service Canada. 2017b. *Commissioner's Directive 009: Research*. Ottawa, Ontario. https://www.csc-scc.gc.ca/acts-and-regulations/009-cd-en.shtml

Crewe, Ben. 2009. *The Prisoner Society: Power, Adaption, and Social Life in an English Prison*. Oxford: Oxford University Press.

Crewe, Ben. 2011. "Depth, Weight, Tightness: Revisiting the Pains of Imprisonment." *Punishment & Society* 13 (5): 509–529.

Crewe, Ben. 2014. "Not Looking Hard Enough: Masculinity, Emotion, and Prison Research." *Qualitative Inquiry* 20 (4): 392–403.

Crewe, Ben, Jason Warr, Peter Bennett, and Alan Smith. 2014. "The Emotional Geography of Prison Life." *Theoretical Criminology* 18 (1): 56–74.

Crewe, Ben, and Alice Ievins. 2020. "The Prison as a Reinventive Institution." *Theoretical Criminology* 24 (4): 568–589.

Day, Rebecca. 2013. *The Experience of 'Journey Woman' from the Perspective of the Participants*. Geese Theatre. https://www.artsevidence.org.uk/media/uploads/research-report-geese-theatre.pdf

Day, Andrew. 2019. "A Correctional Perspective on the Creative Arts in Prisons." In *Performing Arts in Prisons: Creative Perspective*, edited by Michael Balfour, Brydie-Leigh Bartleet, Linda Davey, John Rynne, and Huib Schippers, 21–32. Bristol: Intellect Books.

Davey, Linda. 2019. "Breaking the Fifth Wall: How Performance Might Assist Desistance from Crime." In *Performing Arts in Prisons: Creative Perspective*, edited by Michael Balfour, Brydie-Leigh Bartleet, Linda Davey, John Rynne, and Huib Schippers, 95–114. Bristol: Intellect Books.

Davey, Linda, Andrew Day, and Michael Balfour. 2015. "Performing Desistance: How Might Theories of Desistance from Crime Help Us Understand the Possibilities of Prison Theatre?" *International Journal of Offender Therapy and Comparative Criminology* 59 (8): 798–809.

De Viggiani, Nick. 2012. "Trying to be Something You Are Not: Masculine Performances Within a Prison Setting." *Men and Masculinities* 15 (3): 271–291.

Duguid, Stephen. 1998. "British Columbia Prison Education Research Project. Final Report." Simon Fraser University: Education Resources Information Center. https://files.eric.ed.gov/fulltext/ED419150.pdf

Duriez, Stephanie A., Carrie Sullivan, Edward J. Latessa, and Lori Brusman Lovins. 2018. "The Evolution of Correctional Program Assessment in the Age of Evidence-based Practices." *Corrections* 3 (2): 119–136.

Dworin, Judy. 2011. "Time In: Transforming Identity Inside and Out." In *Performing New Lives: Prison Theatre*, edited by Jonathan Shailor, 83–101. Philadelphia: Jessica Kingsley Publishers.

Ellis, Rachel. 2021. "Prisons as Porous Institutions." *Theory and Society* 50 (2): 175–199.

Evans, Tony, and Patti Wallace. 2008. "A Prison within a Prison? The Masculinity Narratives of Male Prisoners." *Men and Masculinities* 10 (4): 484–507.

Ezzy, Douglas. 2002. *Qualitative Analysis: Practice and Innovation*. Victoria: Routledge.

Farrington, Keith. 1992. "The Modern Prison as Total Institution? Public Perception Versus Objective Reality." *Crime & Delinquency* 38 (1): 6–26.

Ferrell, Jeff, Keith Hayward, and Jock Young. 2008. *Cultural Criminology: An Invitation*. Los Angeles: Sage.

Fesette, Nicholas, Bruce Levitt, and Jayme Kilburn. 2021. "Prison Theatre and the Right to Look." *Research in Drama Education: The Journal of Applied Theatre and Performance* 26 (3): 461–476.

Frauley, Jon. 2015. "On Imaginative Criminology and its Significance." *Societies* 5 (3): 618–630.

Frigon, Sylvie, ed. 2019. *Danse, enfermement et corps résilients / Dance, Confinement and Resilient Bodies*. Ottawa: University of Ottawa Press.

Frigon, Sylvie. 2014. "When Prison Blossoms into Art: Dance in Prison as an Embodied Critical Creative Performative Criminology." In *The Poetics of Crime*, edited by Michael Hviid Jacobsen, 237–262. London: Ashgate Publishing.

Frigon, Sylvie. 2015. "La danse en criminologie : une échappée belle hors de la classe." In *Processus de Création et Processus Cliniques*, edited by Mireille Cifali, Florence Giust-Desprairies, and Thomas Périlleux, 113–135. Paris: Presses Universitaires de France.

Gillespie, Wayne. 2002. *Prisonization: Individual and Institutional Factors Affecting Inmate Conduct*. El Paso: LFB Scholarly Publishing.

Goffman, Erving. 1961. *Asylums: Essay on the Social Situation of Mental Patients and Other Inmates*. New York: Anchor Books.

Goffman, Erving. 1959. *The Presentation of Self in Everyday Life*. New York: Anchor Books.

Government of Canada. 2022. *Tri-Council Policy Statement: Ethical conduct for Research Involving Humans*. https://ethics.gc.ca/eng/policy-politique_tcps2-eptc2_2022.html.

Gray, Ann. 2003. *Research Practice for Cultural Studies*. London: Sage.

Grbich, Carol. 2004. *New Approaches in Social Research*. Thousand Oaks: Sage Publications.

Guba, Egon, and Yvonna Lincoln. 1994. "Competing Paradigms in Qualitative Research." In *The Sage Handbook of Qualitative Research*, edited by Norman Denzin and Yvonna Lincoln, 105–117. Thousand Oaks, CA: Sage Publications.

Guillemin, Marilys, and Lynn Gillam. 2004. "Ethics, Reflexivity, and 'Ethically Important Moments' in Research." *Qualitative Inquiry*, 10 (2): 261–280.

Halperin, Ronnie, Suzanne Kessler, and Dana Braunschweiger. 2012. "Rehabilitation through the Arts: Impact on Participants' Engagement in Educational Programs." *Journal of Correctional Education* 63 (1): 6–23.

Hammersley, Martyn. 2013. *What is Qualitative Research?* New York: Bloomsbury Publishing.

Hammersley, Martyn, and Paul Atkinson. 1983. "Insider Accounts: Listening and Asking Questions." In *Ethnography: Principles in Practice*, 105–126.

Hancock, Philip, and Yvonne Jewkes. 2011. "Architectures of Incarceration: The Spatial Pains of Imprisonment." *Punishment & Society* 13 (5): 611–629.

Haney, Craig. 2011. "The Perversions of Prison: On the Origins of Hypermasculinity and Sexual Violence in Confinement." *American Criminal Law Review* 48 (1): 121–141.

Hazou, Rand, and Reginold Daniels. 2022. "Unshackling the Body, Mind, and Spirit: Reflections on Liberation and Creative Exchange between San Quentin and Auckland Prisons." *Humanities* 11 (7): 1–16.

Hesse-Biber, Sharlene, and Patricia Leavy. 2006. *The Practice of Qualitative Research*. Thousand Oaks: Sage Publications.

Hughes, Jenny. 2005. *Doing the Arts Justice: A Review of Research Literature, Practice and Theory*. The Unit for the Arts and Offenders Centre for Applied Theatre Research. http://www.artsevidence.org.uk/evaluations/doing-arts-justice-review-research-literature-prac/

Irwin, John, and Donald R. Cressey. 1962. "Thieves, Convicts, and the Inmate Culture." *Social Problems* 10 (2): 142–155.

Israel, Mark. 2004. "Strictly Confidential? Integrity and the Disclosure of Criminological and Socio-Legal Research." *British Journal of Criminology* 44 (5): 715–740.

Jacobsen, Michael Hviid, ed. 2014. *The Poetics of Crime: Understanding and Researching Crime and Deviance through Creative Sources*. London: Ashgate Publishing.

Jewkes, Yvonne. 2005. "Men Behind Bars: 'Doing' Masculinity as an Adaptation to Imprisonment." *Men and Masculinities* 8 (1): 44–63.

Johnson, Hanna, Sarah Keen, and David Pritchard. 2011. *Unlocking Value: The Economic Benefit of the Arts in Criminal Justice*. London: New Philanthropy Capital.

Jones, Phil. 2007. *Drama as Therapy: Theory, Practice and Research*. New York: Routledge.

Karp, David. 2010. "Unlocking Men, Unmasking Masculinities: Doing Men's Work in Prison." *The Journal of Men's Studies* 18 (1): 63–83.

Khutan, Ranjit. 2014. "Demonstrating Effectiveness: Competing Discourses in the Use and Evaluation of Applied Theatre that Contributes to Improved Health Outcomes for Prisoners." PhD diss., University of Manchester.

Kincheloe, Joe, and Peter McLaren. 2005. "Rethinking Critical Theory and Qualitative Research." In *The Sage Handbook of Qualitative Research*, edited by Norman Denzin and Yvonna Lincoln, 303–342. Thousand Oaks, CA: Sage Publications.

Kobayashi, Audrey. 2001. "Negotiating the Personal and the Political in Critical Qualitative Research." In *Qualitative Methodologies for Geographers: Issues and Debates*, edited by Melanie Limb and Claire Dwyer, 55–72. New York: Oxford University Press.

Landry, Deborah. 2013. "Are We Human? Edgework in Defiance of the Mundane and Measurable." *Critical Criminology* 21 (1): 1–14.

Landy, Robert. 1996. *Essays in Drama Therapy: The Double Life*. London: Jessica Kingsley.

Langley, Dorothy. 2006. *An Introduction to Dramatherapy*. London: Sage Publications.

Leeder, Abigail, and Colleen Wimmer. 2007. "Voices of Pride: Drama Therapy with Incarcerated Women." *Women & Therapy* 29 (3-4): 195–213.

Link, Bruce, and Jo Phelan. 2001. "Conceptualizing Stigma." *Annual Review of Sociology* 27 (1): 363–385.

Lucas, Ashley. 2020. *Prison Theatre and the Global Crisis of Incarceration*. New York: Bloomsbury Publishing.

Martin, Lauren L., and Matthew L. Mitchelson. 2009. "Geographies of Detention and Imprisonment: Interrogating Spatial Practices of Confinement, Discipline, Law, and State Power." *Geography Compass* 3 (1): 459–477.

Martinson, Robert. 1974. "What Works? Questions and Answers about Prison Reform." *The Public Interest* 35(2): 22–54.

McAvinchey, Caoimhe. 2020. *Applied Theatre: Women and the Criminal Justice System*. London: Bloomsbury Publishing.

McAvinchey, Caoimhe. 2011. *Theatre and Prison*. New York: Palgrave Macmillan.

McGuire, James, ed. 1995. *What Works: Reducing Re-offending: Guidelines from Research and Practice*. Chichester: John Wiley & Sons.

Merrill, Elise. 2015. "Blossoming Bit by Bit: Exploring the Role of Theatre Initiatives in the Lives of Criminalized Women." Master's thesis, University of Ottawa.

Merrill, Elise, and Sylvie Frigon. 2015. "Performative Criminology and the 'State of Play' for Theatre with Criminalized Women." *Societies* 5: 295–313.

Messerschmidt, James. 1993. *Masculinities and Crime: Critique and Reconceptualization of Theory*. Totowa: Rowman & Littlefield Publishers.

Mills, Wright. 1959. *The Sociological Imagination*. New York: Oxford University Press.

Moller, Lorraine. 2003. "A Day in the Life of a Prison Theatre Program." *The Drama Review* 47 (1): 49–73.

Moller, Lorraine. 2013. "Project 'For Colored Girls': Breaking the Shackles of Role Deprivation through Prison Theatre." *The Arts in Psychotherapy* 40 (1): 61–70.

Moran, Dominique. 2013. "Between Outside and Inside? Prison Visiting Rooms as Liminal Carceral Spaces." *GeoJournal* 78 (2): 339–351.

Mortari, Luigina. 2015. "Reflectivity in Research Practice: An Overview of Different Perspectives." *International Journal of Qualitative Methods* 14 (5): 1–9.

Moyes, Jacqui. 2019. "Arts in Corrections New Zealand." In *Performing Arts in Prisons: Creative Perspective*, edited by Michael Balfour, Brydie-Leigh Bartleet, Linda Davey, John Rynne, and Huib Schippers, 133–150. Bristol: Intellect Books.

Munn, Melissa. 2012. "The Mark of Criminality Rejections and Reversals, Disclosure and Distance: Stigma and the Ex-Prisoner." In *Stigma Revisited: Implications of the Mark*, edited by Stacey Hannem and Chris Bruckert, 147–169. Ottawa: University of Ottawa Press.

Nicholson, Helen. 2014. *Applied Drama: The Gift of Theatre*. London: Bloomsbury Publishing.

Neuman, William Lawrence. 2009. *Understanding Research*. New York: Pearson Education.

Newton, Carolyn. 1994. "Gender Theory and Prison Sociology: Using Theories of Masculinities to Interpret the Sociology of Prisons for Men." *The Howard Journal of Criminal Justice* 33 (3): 193–202.

Paulsen, Derek. 2003. "Murder in Black and White: The Newspaper Coverage of Homicide in Houston." *Homicide Studies* 7 (3): 289–317.

Pensalfini, Robert. 2016. *Prison Shakespeare: For These Deep Shames and Great Indignities.* London: Palgrave Macmillan.

Pensalfini, Robert. 2019. "The Play's the Thing: Performance in Prison Shakespeare." In *Performing Arts in Prisons: Creative Perspective*, edited by Michael Balfour, Brydie-Leigh Bartleet, Linda Davey, John Rynne, and Huib Schippers, 151–168. Bristol: Intellect Books.

Phillips, Jenny. 2001. "Cultural Construction of Manhood in Prison." *Psychology of Men & Masculinity* 2 (1): 13–23.

Piamote, Stephanie. 2016. "The Criminological Imagination and the Promise of Fiction." In *C. Wright Mills and the Criminological Imagination*, edited by Jon Frauley, 241–254. New York: Routledge.

Pickett, Justin T., Christina Mancini, and Daniel P. Mears. 2013. "Vulnerable Victims, Monstrous Offenders, and Unmanageable Risk: Explaining Public Opinion on the Social Control of Sex Crime." *Criminology* 51 (3): 729–759.

Pittaway, Eileen, Linda Bartolomei, and Richard Hugman. 2010. "'Stop Stealing Our Stories': The Ethics of Research with Vulnerable Groups." *Journal of Human Rights Practice* 2 (2): 229–251.

Poland, Blake D. 1995. "Transcription Quality as an Aspect of Rigor in Qualitative Research." *Qualitative Inquiry* 1 (3): 290–310.

Prendergast, Monica. 2013. "Running Around with Inmates, Maps and Swords: A Reflective Poetic-Narrative Autoethnography of a Prison Theatre Production." *Research in Drama Education: The Journal of Applied Theatre and Performance* 18 (3): 313–323.

Prendergast, Monica. 2016. "Tracing the Journey to Here: Reflections on a Prison Theatre Devised Project." *Theatre Topics* 26 (3): 343–349.

Presser, Lois. 2004. "Violent Offenders, Moral Selves: Constructing Identities and Accounts in the Research Interview." *Social Problems* 51 (1): 82–101.

Prihar, Neha, and Simon Little. 2014. *History. Act Two: From Cell to Stage. A Radio Documentary*. Last modified April 3, 2014. https://act2doc.wordpress.com/history/

Ricciardelli, Rosemary. 2014a. *Surviving Incarceration: Inside Canadian Prisons*. Waterloo: Wilfrid Laurier University Press.

Ricciardelli, Rosemary. 2014b. "An Examination of the Inmate Code in Canadian Penitentiaries." *Journal of Crime and Justice* 37 (2): 234–255.

Ricciardelli, Rosemary. 2015. "Establishing and Asserting Masculinity in Canadian Penitentiaries." *Journal of Gender Studies* 24 (2): 170–191.

Rogers, Carl. 1945. "The Nondirective Method as a Technique for Social Research." *American Journal of Sociology* 50 (4): 279–283.

Rymhs, Deena. 2012. "In this Inverted Garden: Masculinities in Canadian Prison Writing." *Journal of Gender Studies* 21 (1): 77–89.

Sabo, Donald F., Terry Allen Kupers, and Willie James London, eds. 2001. *Prison Masculinities*. Philadelphia: Temple University Press.

Schlosser, Jennifer A. 2008. "Issues in Interviewing Inmates: Navigating the Methodological Landmines of Prison Research." *Qualitative Inquiry* 14 (8): 1500–1525.

Schwalbe, Michael L., and Michelle Wolkomir. 2003. "Interviewing Men." In *Inside Interviewing: New Lenses, New Concerns*, edited by James Holstein and Jaber Gubrium, 55–71. London: Sage.

Scully, Diana, and Joseph Marolla. 1984. "Convicted Rapists' Vocabulary of Motive: Excuses and Justifications." *Social Problems* 31 (5): 530–544.

Seal, Lizzie and Maggie O'Neill. 2021. *Imaginative Criminology: Of Spaces Past, Present and Future*. Bristol: Bristol University Press.

Serin, Ralph C., Caleb D. Lloyd, and Laura J. Hanby. 2010. "Enhancing Offender Re-entry an Integrated Model for Enhancing Offender Re-entry." *European Journal of Probation* 2(2): 53–75.

Seymour, Kate. 2003. "Imprisoning Masculinity." *Sexuality and Culture* 7 (4): 27–55.

Shailor, Jonathan, ed. 2011. *Performing New Lives: Prison Theatre*. Philadelphia: Jessica Kingsley Publishers.

Siganos, Florine. 2008. *L'action culturelle en prison : Pour une redéfinition du sens de la peine*. Paris: L'Harmattan.

Sim, Joe. 1994. "Tougher than the Rest? Men in Prison." In *Just Boys Doing Business?*, edited by Tim Newburn and Elizabeth Stanko, 100–117. London: Routledge.

Stathopoulos, Alexia. 2023. "Des interventions artistiques en prison pour changer la donne du jeu social carcéral." *Sociographe* 84 (5): LIII–LXXXI.

Sparks, Richard, Anthony Bottoms, and Will Hay. 1996. *Prisons and the Problem of Order*. Oxford: Clarendon.

Sykes, Gresham. 1958. *The Society of Captive: A Study of a Maximum Security Prison*. Princeton: Princeton University Press.

Tett, Lyn, Kirstin Anderson, Fergus McNeill, Katie Overy, and Richard Sparks. 2012. "Learning, Rehabilitation and the Arts in Prisons: A Scottish Case Study." *Studies in the Education of Adults* 44 (2): 171–185.

The North American Drama Therapy Association. n.d. "What Is Drama Therapy?" The North American Drama Therapy Association. Last modified 2023. https://www.nadta.org/what-is-drama-therapy

Thompson, James. 1998. *Prison Theatre: Perspectives & Practices*. London: Jessica Kingsley Publishers.

Thompson, James. 2003. *Applied Theatre: Bewilderment and Beyond*. Bristol: Peter Lang.

Thompson, James. 2009. *Performance Affects: Applied Theatre and the End of Effect*. Basingstoke: Palgrave Macmillan.
Tocci, Laurence. 2007. *The Proscenium Cage: Critical Case Studies in U.S. Prison Theatre Programs*. Youngstown: Cambria Press.
Toch, Hans. 1992. *Living in Prison: The Ecology of Survival*. New York: The Free Press.
Toch, Hans. 1998. "Hyper-masculinity and Prison Violence." In *Masculinities and Violence*, edited by Lee Bowker, 168–178. London: Sage.
Ugelvik, Thomas. 2014. *Power and Resistance in Prison: Doing Time, Doing Freedom*. New York: Springer.
Van den Hoonaard, Deborah. 2012. *Qualitative Research in Action: A Canadian Primer*. Oxford: Oxford University Press.
Waldrop, Deborah. 2004. "Ethical Issues in Qualitative Research with High-Risk Populations." In *The Qualitative Research Experience*, edited by Deborah Padgett, 240–253. Belmont: Thompson, Books and Cole.
Weber, Max. 1905. *The Protestant Ethic and the Spirit of Capitalism*. New York: Scribner.
Weinstein, Raymond M. 1982. "Goffman's Asylums and the Social Situation of Mental Patients." *Orthomolecular Psychiatry* 11(4): 267–274.
William Head on Stage. n.d. *About the Company*. Last modified 2022. https://whonstage.weebly.com/about.html
Woodland, Sarah, and Rand Hazou. 2021. "Carcerality, Theatre, Rights." *Research in Drama Education: The Journal of Applied Theatre and Performance* 26 (3): 385–405.
Young, Jock. 2011. *The Criminological Imagination*. Cambridge: Polity Press.

www.ingramcontent.com/pod-product-compliance
Lightning Source LLC
Jackson TN
JSHW012109200325
81196JS00004B/21